Better Homes and Gardens

BLENDER
COOK BOOK

Blender-chop potatoes for German Potato Pancakes,
then use the blender to prepare golden Fresh Applesauce topping. (See index listing for page.)

BETTER HOMES AND GARDENS BOOKS
Editorial Director: Don Dooley
Managing Editor: Malcolm E. Robinson   Art Director: John Berg
Food Editor: Nancy Morton
Senior Food Editor: Joyce Trollope
Associate Editor: Nancy Byal
Assistant Editors: Pat Olson, Lorene Mundhenke,
Sharyl Heiken, Sandra Wood
Copy Editor: Lawrence Clayton
Designers: George Meininger, Arthur Riser, Julie Zesch

CONTENTS

Better Homes and Gardens
TEST KITCHEN

Our seal assures you that every recipe in Blender Cook Book is endorsed by the Better Homes and Gardens Test Kitchen. Each recipe is tested for family appeal, practicality, and deliciousness.

WHAT YOUR BLENDER WILL DO FOR YOU

Meal preparation is easier and more fun once you "think blender." At the flick of a switch, this versatile kitchen helper trims minutes from cooking jobs while it blends, chops, crumbs, emulsifies, or purees foods to suit your recipe needs. Keep your blender handy where you can use it every time there is a timesaving job it can do.

This includes almost every meal. In each, there is one or more steps that the blender can do faster and easier than you can do it by hand. Even traditional dishes that have always been made the long way around adapt beautifully to the blender. Mexican favorites are good examples. The Guacamole appetizer dip served with corn chips was made velvety smooth in the blender. Likewise, the colorful vegetables and tasty cheese for the Tostadas were blender-chopped one at a time. The layer of Mexican Fried Beans came out of the blender as did the peppy Hot Sauce which gives added flavor and zing.

Recipes you struggled with for years are suddenly no trouble at all when you put the blender to work on them. Think of all the vegetables, fruits, and nuts that no longer need to be chopped by hand. Visualize the delectable salads and desserts in which these foods appear. Bread and cracker crumbs are turned out by the cupful in a few seconds. The same is true of the vanilla wafers or gingersnaps that the blender obligingly converts to crumbs for desserts or piecrusts.

There are numerous recipes that are outstanding when blender-made. Mayonnaise and many types of salad dressing are high on the list. The action of the blender breaks up the oil droplets and disperses them throughout the dressing for a smooth, creamy mixture with great stability. In other types of dressings, the blender distributes the seasonings so that the full flavor is released uniformly.

Soups, gravies, and cream sauces quickly give up their lumps when the blender goes into action. Even hollandaise, long thought to be a very temperamental recipe, is tamed by the rapidly spinning blender.

Beverages were among the first blender foods. Today, they range from milk shake masterpieces to sophisticated cocktails. In between, you will find a bevy of concoctions including frozen juices for breakfast and an array of party punches.

Certain packaged mixes lend themselves to blender techniques. Delicious dips can be prepared from dry mixes plus sour cream or cream cheese thinned with milk. Instant puddings and gelatin mixtures are ready to serve a few minutes after being blender whirled.

Blender action: The first thing to remember about your blender is that it is fast. Even at the lowest speed, seconds make a tremendous difference in the texture of the final product. Although this is most obvious in chopped foods such as cabbage, or in smooth combinations such as those prepared for baby food, it also applies to sauces, salad dressings, appetizer dips, sandwich fillings, and leftovers.

Also remember that the cutting action of the blades does the work. It cuts rather than mixes. When liquid ingredients are present, the whirlpool action within the container draws the larger particles in and out of the blades so that the cutting produces pieces of uniform size. The longer the blender runs, the smaller the pieces will become.

Be sure to read carefully the manufacturer's instruction booklet that comes with your blender. It is the source of valuable

Speedy blender meal

←Serve Hot Sauce with Tostadas filled with meat, cheese, and vegetables including Mexican Fried Beans. Pass Guacamole dip.

Blender tip: Stop blender and use rubber spatula to scrape down sides when blending thick mixtures. Guide the mixture toward the blades for better blending.

Blender tip: Turn on and off quickly when chopping to regulate size of ingredient pieces. Obtain more uniform pieces by breaking or cutting up ingredients first.

information that will help you take advantage of the features of your equipment. While getting acquainted with your blender, you will find it helpful to start and stop the blender often so that you get pieces of the desired fineness. As you become more familiar with the blender's action, choose the speed that is best suited for your recipe's purpose.

There are some things, however, that your blender can't do. The speed and cutting action that makes the blender so versatile limits its use in whipping cream and egg whites. Because the blender cuts food rather than traps air, you will be disappointed in the volume of these foods done in the blender. Also, while the blender will chop cooked meats for leftover creations, its motor is not powerful enough to chop raw meats. Finally, remember that the blender chops rather than whips cooked white potatoes. Texture of blended potato will differ from mashed.

Special techniques: Making the best use of your blender involves a few basic rules. Although much depends upon the specific food involved, here are some techniques that you will use again and again.

1. Cut fresh fruits and vegetables, cooked meats, fish, or seafood into ½- to 1-inch pieces before chopping.

2. Cut firm cheeses in ½-inch pieces. Cube and soften cream cheese before blending with liquid ingredients.

3. Place liquid ingredients into the blender container first unless the recipe instructions say to do otherwise. (Many blender containers are marked in cups and ounces for easy measuring directly into the container.)

4. Do large quantities of foods such as cracker crumbs or raw vegetables in several small batches. It is easier to control the fineness of the pieces and, at the same time, it does not overtax the blender's motor.

BLENDER ARITHMETIC			
Ingredients	Measure	Blender Yield	Hints
Cheese			
Natural (Cheddar, Swiss)	1 cup	1 cup	chop process cheeses with
Process	1 cup	1 cup	½ slice white bread
Crumbs			
Saltine crackers	13-14	½ cup	can do all at one time
White bread	1 slice	¾ cup	tear in pieces
Chocolate wafers	8	½ cup	break in pieces
Graham crackers	6-7	½ cup	break in pieces
Vanilla wafers	12	½ cup	do 6-7 at one time
Zwieback	6-8	½ cup	break in pieces
Fruits			
Apples	1 medium	½ cup	chop wet* or dry
Cranberries	1 cup	1 cup	chop fresh or frozen
Nuts	½ cup	½ cup	chop dry or with other ingredients
Meat, cooked			
All kinds	½ cup	¾ cup	chop dry
Vegetables			
Cabbage	1 medium head	7 cups	chop wet*—(you can fill blender container)
Carrot	1 medium	½ cup	chop dry
Celery	1 medium stalk	⅓ cup	chop wet* or dry
Green Pepper	1 medium	½ cup	chop wet* or dry
Onion	1 small	½ cup	chop wet° or dry
	1 slice	1 tablespoon	chop with other ingredients
Parsley, stemmed	½ cup	¼ cup	chop dry
Miscellaneous			
Eggs, hard-cooked	3	1 cup	chill before chopping
Chocolate, baking	2 ounces	⅓ cup	cut in quarters; add pieces while blender is on
Peppermint candies	8 pieces	¼ cup	can do all at once *see tip, page 43

Add new variety to your menus, yet spend less time in the kitchen. The secret—delegate to your blender an assortment of time-consuming food preparation chores.

There's hardly a meal planned that does not have one or more uses for this handy appliance. Choose a frothy beverage to serve at breakfast, lunch, dinner, or in between. Plan a full-bodied soup, crisp salad, or well-seasoned vegetable to complement a satisfying meat entrée. Make an accompanying dressing or sauce in the blender, too. Surprise your family often with fresh-from-the-oven breads or irresistible desserts.

Emphasis in these recipes is on the good foods blenders produce. Preparing food is easier and more fun with a blender.

Feature golden Stuffed Cornish Hens to be served with Cumberland Sauce at your next special dinner. Complete the meal with Chinese pea pods.

Mealtime shortcuts

EASY THIRST QUENCHERS

Call on your blender often to make refreshing beverages to serve at mealtimes or in between. Begin the day with your favorite fruit juice concentrate, frothy and full-flavored after its spin in the blender. Fill after-school snack requests easily with a blender milk shake, malt, or other milk-based drink.

And don't overlook the family-pleasing beverages based on canned and frozen fruit or vegetable juices combined deliciously with assorted flavorings, spices, soft drink mixes, or fresh bananas or berries.

CRANBERRY-CHERRY COOLER

1 envelope unsweetened cherry-flavored soft drink powder
¼ cup sugar
½ cup orange juice
1 16-ounce bottle cranberry juice cocktail, chilled (2 cups)
  Ice

Combine all ingredients in blender container; blend till drink powder and sugar are dissolved. Serve mixture over ice. Serves 4.

PEACHY-CREAM MILK SHAKE

¼ cup milk
1 cup sliced peaches
1 pint peach ice cream
• • •
¾ cup milk
  Sugar
  Peach slices

Put the ¼ cup milk and sliced peaches in blender container; blend till smooth. Spoon in ice cream. Adjust lid; blend till softened. Add ¾ cup milk; blend till mixture is combined. Sweeten with sugar, if desired. Pour into tall glasses. Garnish each serving with fresh peach slices, if desired. Makes 3 to 4 servings.

STRAWBERRY-LEMON SLUSH

Spruce up favorite old-time lemonade by combining it with fresh pureed strawberries—

3 cups water
1 cup lemon juice
1 cup sugar
2 cups fresh strawberries
  Red food coloring
  Crushed ice
  Sliced strawberries
  Lemon slices

Put *1 cup* of the water, lemon juice, sugar, and 2 cups fresh strawberries in blender container. Adjust lid; blend till the strawberries are pureed and the sugar is completely dissolved.

In a pitcher combine strawberry mixture with remaining 2 cups water and a few drops of red food coloring; mix well. Add crushed ice, sliced strawberries, and lemon slice floaters to strawberry mixture in pitcher. Serves 6.

Instant refreshers

Quench a growing thirst on a hot summer → day with cool and smooth Peachy-Cream Milk Shake or Strawberry-Lemon Slush.

PINEAPPLE-APRICOT CRUSH

   1 12-ounce can pineapple juice, chilled
   1 8¾-ounce can apricot halves, undrained
   6 to 8 ice cubes

Blend first 2 ingredients in blender container till apricots are pureed. Add ice cubes (*see tip, page 69*). Serve at once. Serves 4.

PEAR FLIP

   1 12-ounce can pineapple juice
   1 8-ounce can pear halves, undrained
   2 teaspoons lemon juice
      Few drops peppermint extract
      Mint leaves

Blend first 4 ingredients in blender container till pears are pureed. Serve mixture over ice cubes; garnish with mint leaves. Serves 4 to 5.

GOLDEN SLUSH

   1 12-ounce can peach nectar, chilled
   1 6-ounce can frozen orange juice concentrate
   1 tablespoon lemon juice
   3 cups crushed ice

Put all ingredients in blender container; blend till combined. Makes 3 to 4 servings.

GRAPEFRUIT LIMEADE

   1 18-ounce can grapefruit juice, chilled (2¼ cups)
   1 cup water
   ¾ cup sugar
   1 envelope unsweetened lemon-lime flavored soft drink powder
   2 cups crushed ice

Put first 4 ingredients in blender container; blend till combined. Add ice and blend till mixed. Serve immediately. Serves 4 to 5.

CUCUMBER-TOMATO DRINK

Start a meal with this snappy drink—

   ½ medium cucumber
   1 18-ounce can tomato juice, chilled (2¼ cups)
   2 tablespoons lemon juice
   1 teaspoon onion salt
      Few drops bottled hot pepper sauce
      Ice cubes
      Cucumber sticks

Peel cucumber; halve lengthwise and remove seeds. Cut cucumber in pieces. Put cucumber pieces and next 4 ingredients in blender container; blend till cucumber is pureed and ingredients are combined. Serve over ice cubes, with cucumber stick stirrers. Serves 5 to 6.

TOMATO SOUP-KRAUT DRINK

   1 10¾-ounce can condensed tomato soup
   1 cup sauerkraut juice
  12 ice cubes

Put condensed tomato soup and sauerkraut juice in blender container; blend till combined. Add ice cubes, one at a time, till chopped (*see tip, page 69*). Makes 8 servings.

RASPBERRY FROTH

Use flavored gelatin to make this easy drink—

   1 3-ounce package raspberry-flavored gelatin
   ½ cup boiling water
   1 10-ounce package red raspberries, partially thawed
  1½ cups cold milk
   1 cup crushed ice

Put gelatin and boiling water in blender container; blend till gelatin is dissolved. Add partially thawed raspberries, cold milk, and crushed ice; blend till ice dissolves. Serve immediately. Makes 4 to 5 servings.

Blender tip: Spoon ice cream or sherbet, a small amount at a time, into the liquid ingredients in blender container. Blend till mixture is smooth after each addition.

ORANGE-BERRY WAKE-UP

Begin the day or end an evening with this nutritious beverage and snack—

    1 cup orange juice
    1 egg
    1 10-ounce package frozen
        strawberries, partially thawed
    ½ cup non-fat dry milk powder
    ½ cup cold water
        Orange twists
        Fresh strawberries

Put orange juice, egg, package of partially thawed strawberries, non-fat dry milk powder, and cold water in the blender container. Blend till the mixture is smooth. Pour strawberry mixture into 4 glasses; garnish each serving with an orange twist and a fresh strawberry. Serve immediately. Serves 4.

CHOCOLATE-BANANA SPECIAL

    1 medium banana
    2 cups cold chocolate-flavored milk
    ¼ teaspoon vanilla

Peel banana; cut into 1-inch pieces. Wrap banana in foil; freeze solid. Place chocolate milk, frozen pieces of banana, and vanilla in blender container. Blend till the banana is pureed and ingredients are combined. Makes 3 servings.

SPICED PRUNE DRINK

    1 cup prune juice, chilled
    1 8-ounce carton plain yogurt
    ⅓ cup confectioners' sugar
    ¼ teaspoon ground cinnamon

Combine all ingredients in blender container; blend till combined. Makes 2 to 3 servings.

BUTTERMILK BLUSH

    2 cups cold buttermilk
    2 nectarines, chilled, peeled, and
        cut in pieces
    ¼ cup brown sugar

Combine all ingredients in blender container; blend till the nectarines are pureed. Serve mixture in chilled glasses. Makes 4 servings.

GRAPE FROTH

    1 6-ounce can frozen grape juice
        concentrate
    2 juice cans water (1½ cups)
    1 pint lemon sherbet
    1 16-ounce bottle lemon-lime
        carbonated beverage, chilled

Put frozen grape juice concentrate and water in blender container; spoon in lemon sherbet. Blend till mixture is smooth. Pour 1 cup grape mixture into each of 4 tall glasses; slowly add ½ cup chilled carbonated beverage to each glass. Stir mixture gently. Makes 4 servings.

STRAWBERRY FROSTY

1 3-ounce package strawberry-
   flavored gelatin
1 cup boiling water
1 quart cold milk
1 quart strawberry ice cream
   Fresh strawberries

Put strawberry-flavored gelatin and boiling water in blender container; blend at low speed till gelatin is dissolved. Pour ½ *cup* of the gelatin mixture into measuring cup; set aside.

Add *half* the milk to remaining mixture in blender container; blend on low speed till mixed. Add *half* the strawberry ice cream; blend till smooth. Pour into tall glasses. Repeat with reserved gelatin mixture, milk, and ice cream. Garnish each glass with a fresh strawberry, if desired. Makes 6 servings.

MALTED MILK

1 cup cold milk
¼ cup chocolate syrup *or* other
   syrup flavor
2 tablespoons malted milk powder
1 pint vanilla ice cream

Put cold milk, syrup, and malted milk powder in blender container; spoon in ice cream. Blend till mixture is smooth. Makes 3 servings.

FRESH STRAWBERRY MALT

As pictured on the cover—

¾ to 1 cup cold milk
2 tablespoons malted milk powder
1 cup fresh strawberries
1 tablespoon sugar
1 pint vanilla ice cream
   Fresh strawberries

Put cold milk, malted milk powder, fresh strawberries, and sugar in blender container; spoon in vanilla ice cream. Blend till mixture is smooth. Garnish with additional fresh strawberries, if desired. Makes 3 servings.

APPLE EGGNOG

3 eggs
   Dash ground cinnamon
   Dash ground ginger
2 cups apple juice, chilled
1 pint vanilla ice cream
   Ground nutmeg

Put first 4 ingredients in blender container; blend till mixed. Spoon in ice cream; blend till smooth. Top with nutmeg. Serves 6 to 8.

STRAWBERRY-BANANA SHAKE

1 cup cold milk
1 medium banana, cut in pieces
1 pint strawberry ice cream

Put milk and banana in blender container; add ice cream. Blend smooth. Serves 2 to 3.

CHERRY SHAKE

1 21-ounce can cherry pie filling
1 quart vanilla ice cream
2 cups cold milk
   Peppermint sticks

In blender container put *half* of the cherry pie filling. Spoon in *half* of the ice cream; pour in *half* of the milk. Adjust lid; blend till ingredients are combined. Pour mixture into tall serving glasses. Repeat process with remaining cherry pie filling, ice cream, and milk. Use peppermint sticks for muddlers, if desired. Makes 4 or 5 servings.

BANANA-APRICOT SHAKE

½ cup cold milk
1 cup apricot nectar, chilled
1 cup vanilla ice cream
1 small banana, cut in pieces
2 drops almond extract

Put ingredients in blender container; blend till smooth. Makes 2 generous servings.

MOCHA-CREAM SHAKE

2½ cups cold milk
4 teaspoons instant coffee powder
½ cup chocolate syrup
1 quart chocolate ice cream

Put *1 cup* of milk, coffee powder, and syrup in blender container; spoon in ice cream. Blend smooth. Add rest of milk; blend. Serves 6.

TROPICAL HOT CHOCOLATE

1 quart milk
6 tablespoons presweetened instant cocoa powder
1 large banana, cut in pieces
½ teaspoon vanilla
Marshmallows

Blend *1 cup* of milk, cocoa, and banana in blender till smooth. Heat with vanilla and rest of milk. Top with marshmallows. Serves 4.

HOT COFFEE ALOHA

2 cups milk
2 tablespoons sugar
1⅛ cups flaked coconut
2 cups extra-strong coffee
Whipped cream
Toasted coconut

Heat first 3 ingredients together. Put in blender container; blend till smooth. Strain. Add coffee; reheat. Top each serving with whipped cream and toasted coconut. Makes 4 servings.

LEMON-TEA FROSTY

3 cups cold water
2 tablespoons instant tea powder
1 6-ounce can frozen lemonade concentrate
1 pint lemon sherbet

Put all ingredients in blender container; blend till combined. Makes 5 servings.

Float big scoops of lime sherbet atop Frosty Lime Fizz before serving to the back-yard barbecue gang on a warm afternoon.

FROSTY LIME FIZZ

Add half the lime sherbet to the pineapple and lime juice mixture in blender container—

1 12-ounce can pineapple juice chilled (1½ cups)
½ cup lime juice
½ cup sugar
1 quart lime sherbet
1 28-ounce bottle lemon-lime carbonated beverate, chilled

Put pineapple juice, lime juice, and sugar in blender container; spoon *half* of the lime sherbet into blender container. Adjust lid; blend till ingredients are smooth.

Pour ½ cup of the pineapple-lime mixture into each of six 12-ounce glasses. Add an additional scoop of lime sherbet to each glass. Fill each glass with chilled lemon-lime carbonated beverage. Makes 6 servings.

BLENDER-FAST SALADS AND SALAD DRESSINGS

Let your blender take over the time-consuming tasks in saladmaking. It will do a salad bowlful of chopped vegetables in a matter of seconds, and gelatin for molded salads is dissolved in record time.

No truly superb salad is complete until it is suitably dressed. The blender's speed is uniquely suited for distributing flavors and emulsifying the mixture into a dressing worthy of the salad beneath it.

GARDEN ROW SALAD

  3 medium carrots, sliced
  1 large cucumber
  1 pint cherry tomatoes, halved
  4 stalks celery, sliced
1½ cups croutons
  4 ounces sharp natural Cheddar
      cheese, cut in cubes (1 cup)
  ½ slice bread, torn in pieces
  2 hard-cooked eggs, sliced
  6 slices bacon, crisp-cooked and
      crumbled
    Choice of salad dressing

Put carrots in blender container; cover with *cold* water. Blend till coarsely chopped. Drain. Layer carrots in bottom of glass salad bowl.

Halve cucumber lengthwise; remove seeds. Cut cucumber in pieces; put in blender container. Cover with *cold* water. Blend till coarsely chopped. Drain. Layer cucumber atop carrots. Place tomatoes atop cucumbers.

Put celery in blender container; cover with *cold* water. Blend till coarsely chopped. Drain; layer celery atop tomatoes. Place croutons atop celery layer in bowl.

Wipe blender container dry. Put cheese and bread in blender container; blend till coarsely chopped. Arrange cheese, egg slices, and bacon atop salad. Before serving, toss with dressing. Makes 10 to 12 servings.

MENU

Oven Parmesan Chicken*
Buttered Peas
Garden Row Salad*
Assorted Dressings
Hot Rolls   Butter
Orange-Pecan Pie*
Beverage

*See index listing for page number.

BASIC BLENDER COLESLAW

  3 stalks celery, sliced
  ½ green pepper, cut in pieces
  2 green onions, sliced
  1 small head cabbage, cored and
      cut in small wedges
  1 cup dairy sour cream
  ¼ cup tarragon vinegar
  2 tablespoons sugar
  1 teaspoon salt

Put *half* the vegetables in blender container in order listed; add *cold* water to cover. Blend till coarsely chopped. Drain. Repeat with remaining vegetables; chill. Put dairy sour cream, vinegar, sugar, and salt in container; blend till combined. Chill. Before serving, drain vegetables again and toss lightly with sour cream mixture. Makes 8 servings.

Salad in the round

Toss colorful Garden Row Salad with your → favorite salad dressing—Italian Dressing, French Dressing, or Blender Mayonnaise.

FRUITED COLESLAW

    1 small head cabbage
    1 medium apple, unpeeled
    1 8¾-ounce can pineapple tidbits
    ¾ cup seedless green grapes, halved
    ¾ cup salad oil
    ¼ cup lime juice
    1 tablespoon vinegar
    ⅓ cup sugar

Core cabbage and cut into small wedges. Cut apple in quarters; core. Combine *half* the cabbage and all the apple in blender container; add *cold* water to cover. Adjust lid; blend till coarsely chopped. Drain. Repeat with remaining cabbage. Drain pineapple, reserving syrup. Toss together chopped apple and cabbage, pineapple, and grapes; chill.

Just before serving put reserved pineapple syrup, salad oil, lime juice, vinegar, and sugar in blender container; blend till combined. Pour desired amount of dressing over coleslaw; toss lightly. Makes 6 servings.

SPECIAL SPINACH SALAD

    4 ounces sharp natural Cheddar cheese, cut in cubes (1 cup)
    ½ cup salad oil
    ⅓ cup wine vinegar
    3 hard-cooked eggs, quartered
    2 green onions, sliced
    1 teaspoon sugar
    ½ teaspoon garlic salt
    ½ teaspoon salt
    ¼ teaspoon pepper
    8 cups torn fresh spinach *or* escarole
    2 slices bacon, crisp-cooked and crumbled

Put cheese in blender container; blend till coarsely chopped. Remove and set aside. Put salad oil, wine vinegar, eggs, green onion, sugar, garlic salt, salt, and pepper in blender container; blend till egg and onion are chopped. Stir egg mixture and chopped cheese together; chill. Toss dressing with spinach; top with bacon. Makes 6 servings.

CARROT-FRUIT SLAW

    1 medium apple, unpeeled
    3 medium carrots, sliced
    3 medium oranges, peeled and diced
    ½ cup raisins
    ¾ cup mayonnaise or salad dressing
       Lettuce cups

Cut apple in quarters; remove core. Put apple and sliced carrots in blender container; cover with *cold* water. Adjust lid; blend till apple and carrots are coarsely chopped. Drain.

In large bowl combine chopped apple and carrot mixture, oranges, raisins, and mayonnaise or salad dressing; toss lightly. Chill before serving. Serve salad mixture in lettuce cups. Makes 6 cups.

CAULIFLOWER-OLIVE TOSS

    1 small head cauliflower (about 1 pound)
    ½ cup salad oil
    ¼ cup lemon juice
    ½ small onion, cut in pieces
    ¼ cup pimiento-stuffed green olives
    1 teaspoon salt
    ¼ teaspoon pepper
       • • •
    2 ounces sharp natural Cheddar cheese, cut in cubes (½ cup)
    4 cups torn romaine

Separate cauliflower into flowerets. Cook, covered, in small amount of boiling, salted water just till crisp-tender, about 10 minutes; drain. Slice larger cauliflowerets; place flowerets in deep bowl.

Put salad oil, lemon juice, onion, pimiento-stuffed olives, salt, and pepper in blender container. Adjust lid; blend till onion and olives are coarsely chopped. Pour mixture over cauliflower in deep bowl. Chill at least 2 or 3 hours, stirring frequently.

Put cheese in blender container. Adjust lid; blend till cheese is coarsely chopped. Just before serving toss marinated mixture with torn romaine. Top with chopped Cheddar cheese. Makes 6 servings.

BEAN BONANZA SALAD

1 16-ounce can kidney beans, drained
1 16-ounce can cut wax beans, drained
1 16-ounce can cut green beans,
   drained
1 16-ounce can green lima beans,
   drained
½ cup sugar
½ cup salad oil
½ cup wine vinegar
½ medium onion, cut in pieces
1 small green pepper, cut in pieces
1 teaspoon salt
½ teaspoon dry mustard
½ teaspoon dried tarragon leaves,
   crushed
½ teaspoon dried basil leaves,
   crushed
¼ teaspoon pepper

In large bowl combine drained beans. In blender container place sugar, salad oil, wine vinegar, onion, green pepper, salt, dry mustard, dried tarragon, dried basil, and pepper. Blend till onion and green pepper are finely chopped. Pour salad oil mixture over beans; toss to coat. Chill several hours, stirring occasionally. Makes 8 to 10 servings.

BLUSHING SHRIMP CUPS

3 large tomatoes, chilled and halved
2 stalks celery, sliced
¼ cup mayonnaise or salad dressing
¼ cup dairy sour cream
½ teaspoon prepared horseradish
¼ teaspoon salt
2 4½-ounce cans shrimp, drained and
   cut up
Thinly sliced green onion

Scoop pulp from tomatoes, reserving ⅓ cup. Put reserved pulp in blender container with celery, mayonnaise or salad dressing, dairy sour cream, prepared horseradish, and salt. Blend till celery is coarsely chopped. Toss chopped celery mixture with shrimp. Spoon shrimp mixture into tomato cups. Garnish with green onion. Makes 6 servings.

MACARONI-TUNA SALAD

1 cup corkscrew macaroni
1 medium dill pickle
½ small onion
1 stalk celery, sliced
1 slice bread, torn in pieces
2 ounces process American cheese, cut
   in cubes (½ cup)
2 hard-cooked eggs, quartered
8 small pimiento-stuffed green olives
1 6½- or 7-ounce can tuna, drained
   and flaked
⅔ cup mayonnaise or salad dressing
1 tablespoon lemon juice

Cook macaroni according to package directions. Drain; place in large bowl. Put dill pickle, onion, and celery in blender container; blend till coarsely chopped. Combine with macaroni. Put bread, cheese, eggs, and olives in blender container; blend till coarsely chopped. Mix cheese mixture and tuna with macaroni; chill. Combine mayonnaise or salad dressing and lemon juice. Toss with tuna mixture. Makes 4 to 6 servings.

HAM-PINEAPPLE SALAD

8 ounces fully cooked ham, cut in
   cubes (1½ cups)
2 ounces natural Swiss cheese, cut
   in cubes (½ cup)
   • • •
4 cups torn lettuce
1 cup seedless green grapes, halved
1 8-ounce can crushed pineapple
1 cup cream-style cottage cheese
2 tablespoons lemon juice

Put ham and cheese in blender container; blend till coarsely chopped. In large bowl combine lettuce, grapes, and chopped ham mixture. Toss lightly; chill salad mixture.

Drain pineapple, reserving ¼ cup syrup. Put cottage cheese, crushed pineapple, reserved pineapple syrup, and lemon juice in blender container; blend till smooth. Pour desired amount of dressing over greens. Toss to mix. Makes 4 servings.

BLENDER CUCUMBER SALAD

> 1 large cucumber, peeled
> 1 3-ounce package lemon-flavored gelatin
> 1¼ cups boiling water
> Carrot curls
> Cottage Cheese Dressing

Halve cucumber lengthwise and remove seeds; Adjust lid; blend till cucumber is pureed. (When necessary, stop blender and use rubber spatula to scrape down sides.) Measure cucumber; add water, if necessary, to make 1 cup.

Dissolve gelatin in boiling water; add pureed cucumber. Chill till partially thickened, stirring occasionally. Pour into 3½-cup ring mold. Chill till set. Unmold the salad; fill the center with the carrot curls. Then serve the salad with the Cottage Cheese Dressing. Makes 4 to 6 servings.

AVOCADO SALAD RING

> 1 3-ounce package lemon-flavored gelatin
> 1¼ cups boiling water
> 1 cup dairy sour cream
> ½ cup mayonnaise or salad dressing
> 2 medium avocados, peeled and cut in cubes
> ½ small onion
> 1 tablespoon lemon juice
> ½ teaspoon salt
> 4 to 6 drops green food coloring
> Lettuce
> Orange sections
> Grapefruit sections
> Blender Mayonnaise

Put gelatin in blender container; add boiling water. Adjust lid; blend at low speed till gelatin is dissolved. Add sour cream, mayonnaise, avocado, onion, lemon juice, and salt to gelatin in blender container; blend till smooth. Add food coloring, if desired. Pour into 4½- to 5½-cup ring mold. Chill till firm. Unmold on lettuce; fill center with orange and grapefruit sections. Serve with Blender Mayonnaise. Serves 6 to 8.

Heap crisp carrot curls in center of Blender Cucumber Salad and serve with creamy blender-made Cottage Cheese Dressing.

COTTAGE CHEESE DRESSING

Toss crisp green and vegetable salads or molded and fresh fruit salads with this creamy dressing—

> 1 cup cream-style cottage cheese
> 2 tablespoons sugar
> 4 teaspoons lemon juice
> • • •
> 2 tablespoons milk

Put cream-style cottage cheese, sugar, and lemon juice in blender container; adjust lid and blend till mixture is creamy. Add milk, a tablespoon at a time, and blend till desired consistency is reached.

FRESH TOMATO ASPIC

    4 medium tomatoes, peeled and cut
        in quarters
      Red food coloring
    2 stalks celery, sliced
    ¼ small onion
    2 tablespoons brown sugar
    2 tablespoons lemon juice
    ½ teaspoon salt
    ½ teaspoon celery salt
      Dash bottled hot pepper sauce
    2 envelopes unflavored gelatin
        (2 tablespoons)
    ¾ cup cold water

Put tomatoes in blender container; blend till pureed. Add a few drops red food coloring, if desired. Add celery, onion, brown sugar, lemon juice, salt, celery salt, and hot pepper sauce to blender container. Blend till vegetables are finely chopped.

In small saucepan soften gelatin in cold water. Place over low heat and stir till gelatin is dissolved. Add to tomato mixture; chill till partially set. Turn into 4½-cup ring mold. Chill till firm. Makes 8 servings.

CHEESY-LIME MOLD

    1 3-ounce package lime-flavored
        gelatin
    1¼ cups boiling water
    1 3-ounce package cream cheese,
        cut in cubes and softened
    ½ cup mayonnaise or salad dressing
    1 tablespoon lemon juice
    1 medium cucumber, peeled
    ¼ medium green pepper

Put gelatin and boiling water in blender container; blend at low speed till gelatin is dissolved. Add cream cheese, mayonnaise, and lemon juice to blender container; blend smooth.

Halve cucumber lengthwise; remove seeds and cut in pieces. Add cucumber and green pepper to blender container; blend till coarsely chopped. Chill till partially set, stirring occasionally. Turn into 3½-cup mold. Chill till firm. Makes 6 servings.

GOLDEN SALAD RING

    1 16-ounce can orange and grapefruit
        sections
    1 13¼-ounce can crushed pineapple
    2 3-ounce packages orange-flavored
        gelatin
    1½ cups boiling water
    1 6-ounce can frozen orange juice
        concentrate, thawed
    2 carrots, sliced

Drain fruits, reserving 1½ cups of the combined syrups. Cut up grapefruit and orange sections. Put gelatin in blender container; add 1½ cups boiling water. Blend on low speed to dissolve gelatin. Add orange juice concentrate and reserved syrup to gelatin mixture in blender container; blend to combine. Remove mixture from blender container; chill in refrigerator till partially set.

Put carrots in blender container; blend till carrots are coarsely chopped.

Fold carrots and fruit into gelatin mixture. Turn into 6½-cup ring mold. Chill till firm. Makes 8 to 10 servings.

APRICOT-ORANGE MOLD

    2 3-ounce packages orange-flavored
        gelatin
    2 cups boiling water
    1 11-ounce can mandarin orange
        sections
    1 17-ounce can apricot halves
    ⅓ cup pecans
    2 tablespoons lemon juice
    ½ teaspoon salt

Put gelatin in blender container; add boiling water. Blend on low speed to dissolve gelatin. Drain oranges, reserving liquid. Set oranges aside. Add reserved liquid, apricot halves, pecans, lemon juice, and salt to mixture in blender container; blend just till pecans are chopped. Remove from blender container. Chill till partially set; fold in orange sections. Turn mixture into 6½-cup mold or ten to twelve individual ½-cup molds. Chill till firm. Makes 10 to 12 servings.

TUNA-DRESSED SALAD

1 9-ounce package frozen cut green beans
1 6½- or 7-ounce can tuna, drained
1 cup dairy sour cream
¼ cup mayonnaise or salad dressing
¼ cup chili sauce
2 tablespoons lemon juice
½ teaspoon Worcestershire sauce
¼ teaspoon dry mustard
¼ teaspoon dried oregano leaves,
    crushed
2 cups torn lettuce
4 cups cubed cooked potatoes, chilled
4 ounces natural Swiss cheese, cut in
    2-inch strips (1 cup)
1 tomato, cut in wedges
½ cup courtons
    Paprika

Prepare frozen cut green beans according to package directions; drain and chill.

Put drained tuna, dairy sour cream, mayonnaise or salad dressing, chili sauce, lemon juice, Worcestershire sauce, dry mustard, and oregano in blender container; adjust lid and blend till smooth. Chill.

Line a large salad bowl with torn lettuce. Arrange chilled potatoes, green beans, Swiss cheese, and tomato wedges atop lettuce. Season to taste with salt and pepper.

Spoon chilled tuna dressing over salad; toss to coat. Sprinkle salad with croutons and paprika. Makes 4 to 6 servings.

Special cooking hint: Make good use of leftovers with this recipe. Substitute canned or leftover green beans for the package frozen cut green beans. Other favorite combinations such as asparagus and carrots can also be used.

Whirl a can of drained tuna with sour cream, mayonnaise, and seasonings to be poured over chilled vegetables and cheese strips for Tuna-Dressed Salad.

BLENDER MAYONNAISE

1 large egg
1 tablespoon vinegar
½ teaspoon salt
¼ teaspoon dry mustard
⅛ teaspoon paprika
Dash cayenne
• • •
1 cup salad oil
1 tablespoon lemon juice

Put egg, vinegar, salt, dry mustard, paprika, and cayenne in blender container; blend till mixed. With blender running slowly, gradually pour *half* of the salad oil into blender container. (When necessary, stop blender and use rubber spatula to scrape down sides.)

Add lemon juice to mixture in blender container and slowly pour remainder of salad oil into blender container with the blender running slowly. Makes about 1¼ cups.

THOUSAND ISLAND DRESSING

1 cup mayonnaise or salad dressing
¼ cup chili sauce
2 hard-cooked eggs, quartered
¼ medium green pepper
½ medium stalk celery, sliced
¼ small onion
1 teaspoon paprika
½ teaspoon salt

Put ingredients in blender container; blend till combined and green pepper, celery, and onion are finely chopped. Makes 2 cups.

CAVALIER DRESSING

1 cup mayonnaise or salad dressing
2 tablespoons crumbled blue cheese
1 tablespoon catsup
1 tablespoon vinegar
1 small piece of onion

Put all ingredients in blender container; blend till smooth. Allow to chill at least 30 minutes before serving. Makes 1 cup.

GREEN GODDESS DRESSING

1 cup mayonnaise
½ cup dairy sour cream
1 sprig parsley
1 2-ounce can anchovy fillets, drained
2 tablespoons tarragon vinegar
1 tablespoon lemon juice
Dash pepper

Put all ingredients in blender container; blend till smooth. (When necessary, stop blender and use rubber spatula to scrape down sides.) Makes 1¾ cups.

COTTAGE-HERB DRESSING

1 tablespoon milk
1 12-ounce carton cream-style cottage cheese
1 teaspoon lemon juice
1 thin slice of onion
3 radishes, halved
1 teaspoon mixed salad herbs, crushed
1 sprig parsley
¼ teaspoon salt

Put milk, cottage cheese, and lemon juice in blender container; blend till smooth. Add remaining ingredients to cottage cheese mixture in blender container; blend till vegetables are chopped. Chill. Makes 1½ cups.

CUCUMBER DRESSING

½ medium cucumber
1 cup dairy sour cream
2 tablespoons lemon juice
2 tablespoons sugar
½ teaspoon salt
Dash bottled hot pepper sauce

Halve cucumber lengthwise; remove seeds and cut cucumber in pieces. Add to blender container with remaining ingredients; blend till cucumber is finely chopped. (When necessary, stop blender and use rubber spatula to scrape down sides.) Chill, if desired. Makes 2 cups.

FRENCH DRESSING

½ cup salad oil
2 tablespoons vinegar
2 tablespoons lemon juice
2 teaspoons sugar
½ teaspoon salt
½ teaspoon dry mustard
½ teaspoon paprika
Dash cayenne

Put all ingredients in blender container; blend till combined. Chill. Shake dressing just before serving. Makes ¾ cup.

CREAMY FRENCH DRESSING

⅓ cup vinegar
1 egg
1 tablespoon paprika
1 tablespoon sugar
1 teaspoon salt
Dash cayenne
1 cup salad oil

Put vinegar, egg, paprika, sugar, salt, and dash cayenne in blender container; blend till combined. With blender running slowly, gradually pour salad oil in blender container. Chill. Makes about 1⅔ cups.

FRENCH-CHEESE DRESSING

1 cup salad oil
⅓ cup white wine vinegar
1 teaspoon sugar
1 teaspoon salt
½ teaspoon paprika
Dash pepper
½ clove garlic
¼ small onion
3 ounces blue cheese

Put all ingredients except blue cheese in blender container; blend till onion is finely chopped. Crumble blue cheese into blender container; blend till cheese is chopped. Store in refrigerator. Shake salad dressing mixture before serving over salad. Makes 2 cups.

ITALIAN DRESSING

1 cup salad oil
¼ cup vinegar
1 clove garlic, minced
1 teaspoon salt
½ teaspoon white pepper
½ teaspoon celery salt
¼ teaspooon cayenne
¼ teaspoon dry mustard
Dash bottled hot pepper sauce

Put all ingredients in blender container; blend till combined. Chill thoroughly. Shake before using. Makes 1¼ cups.

ITALIAN-CHEESE DRESSING

Dress up your favorite tossed salad with this Parmesan cheese version of Italian dressing—

1⅓ cups salad oil
½ cup vinegar
¼ cup grated Parmesan cheese
1 tablespoon sugar
2 teaspoons salt
1 teaspoon celery salt
½ teaspoon white pepper
½ teaspoon dry mustard
¼ teaspoon paprika
1 clove garlic, minced

Put all ingredients in blender container; blend till combined. Chill. Makes 1¾ cups.

PEPPY TOMATO DRESSING

1 8-ounce can tomatoes, drained
1 cup salad oil
⅓ cup white wine vinegar
1 slice of onion
½ clove garlic, minced
½ teaspoon salt
¼ teaspoon pepper
¼ teaspoon celery seed

Chop tomatoes; put in blender container with remaining ingredients. Blend till ingredients are well combined. Makes 1¾ cups.

Blender tip: Make creamy dressings by pouring oil, in a slow stream, into blender container with the blender slowly running. Add the oil through the opening in the lid if blender has a removable cover insert.

CONFETTI DRESSING

Stir dressing before serving so tiny bits of onion, olive, green pepper, and celery are dispersed throughout the zippy dressing—

    1 cup salad oil
    ¾ cup vinegar
    ⅛ cup sugar
    1 teaspoon salt
    2 green onions with tops, sliced
    ¼ cup pimiento-stuffed green olives
    ½ small green pepper, cut in pieces
    1 stalk celery, sliced

Put all of the ingredients into the blender container; blend till vegetables are finely chopped. Chill mixture. Stir the mixture before using. Spoon mixture over salad greens. Makes approximately 2⅓ cups dressing.

SNAPPY SALAD DRESSING

    1 cup French salad dressing
    ½ cup dairy sour cream
    1 medium green pepper, cut in
        pieces
    Dash chili powder

Put ingredients in blender container; blend till green pepper is chopped. Makes 1¾ cups.

CHERRY FRENCH DRESSING

    1 4-ounce jar maraschino cherries,
        undrained
    ¼ cup salad oil
    2 tablespoons lemon juice
    2 tablespoons sugar
    ⅛ teaspoon salt

Put ingredients in blender container; blend till cherries are finely chopped. Chill. Shake before using. Makes ¾ cup.

FRUIT SALAD DRESSING

    ⅓ cup orange juice
    ½ teaspoon grated orange peel
    ¼ cup mayonnaise or salad dressing
    1 tablespoon sugar
    1 3-ounce package cream cheese, cut
        in cubes and softened
    Dash cayenne

Put ingredients in blender container; blend till smooth. Makes 1 cup.

HONEY-APRICOT DRESSING

    1 8¾-ounce can unpeeled apricot
        halves, drained
    1 cup dairy sour cream
    ¼ cup honey
    1 tablespoon lemon juice
    Dash salt

Put ingredients in blender container; blend till smooth. Chill, if desired. Makes 1¾ cups.

QUICK SOUPS AND SAUCES

The blender's whirling blades smooth out lumps and greatly simplify soup and sauce making. Try pureeing cooked vegetables to give a full-bodied smoothness to a variety of thick and hearty soups. Remember, too, that even soups containing pieces of vegetable—blender chopped, of course—need a smooth, well-seasoned broth or sauce background for greatest eating enjoyment.

Blend before cooking is the rule in the sauce department. This rule also holds true when you are making a rich gravy with pan drippings from a roast.

MENU

Blender Gazpacho*
Croutons   Cucumber Slices
Hard Rolls
Assorted Meat and Cheese Platter
Baked Custard
Hot Beverage

*See index listing for page number.

BLENDER GAZPACHO

    3 cups tomato juice
    2 tablespoons olive *or* salad oil
    2 tablespoons wine vinegar
    1 clove garlic
    2 medium tomatoes, peeled and
          quartered
    1 small cucumber, cut in pieces
    1 small green pepper, cut in pieces
    3 medium stalks celery, sliced
    ¼ medium onion, cut in pieces
    4 sprigs parsley
    2 slices bread, torn in pieces
    1 teaspoon salt
    ¼ teaspoon freshly ground pepper
    1 cup croutons
       Cucumber slices

Put *1 cup* of the tomato juice, olive or salad oil, wine vinegar, and garlic in blender container. Blend till garlic is finely chopped.

Add *half each* of the tomato, cucumber, green pepper, celery, onion, parsley, bread, salt, and pepper to blender container. Blend till vegetables are pureed. Transfer to 2-quart container. Repeat with remaining tomato juice, vegetables, bread, and seasonings. Cover and chill thoroughly in the refrigerator. Serve in chilled mugs or bowls topped with croutons and cucumber slices. Serves 6.

CHILLED AVO-MATO SOUP

Begin a meal with this ideal appetizer soup—

    1 10½-ounce can condensed beef broth
    2 avocados, peeled and cut in cubes
    ½ cup dairy sour cream
    1 green onion, sliced
    1 teaspoon salt
    1 tablespoon lemon juice
       Dash bottled hot pepper sauce
                • • •
    3 medium tomatoes, peeled and cut up
       Dairy sour cream
       Chopped green onion tops

Put condensed beef broth, avocados, dairy sour cream, green onion, salt, lemon juice, and bottled hot pepper sauce in blender container; blend till smooth. Stir in tomatoes. Chill thoroughly before serving. Garnish with additional dairy sour cream and chopped green onion tops. Makes 4 to 6 servings.

Informal party idea

Offer soup spoons to your guests when you → serve cool and colorful Blender Gazpacho. Garnish with cucumbers and croutons.

VICHYSSOISE

1 10¼-ounce can frozen condensed
    cream of potato soup, thawed
1 10½-ounce can condensed cream of
    chicken soup
1 soup-can milk
1 cup light cream
  Chives

Put first 3 ingredients in blender container; blend till smooth. Add light cream; blend to combine. Chill, covered, 3 to 4 hours or overnight. (If desired, blend again just before serving.) Snip chives over soup. Makes 5 servings.

SHRIMP BISQUE

2½ cups milk
 2 tablespoons butter or margarine
 1 tablespoon all-purpose flour
 1 4½-ounce can shrimp, drained
 ¼ teaspoon dry mustard
   Dash salt
   Dash pepper

Put ingredients in blender container; blend till shrimp is coarsely chopped. Cook, stirring occasionally, till thick and bubbly. Serves 4.

CREAM OF ASPARAGUS SOUP

¾ cup water
¾ teaspoon salt
1 pound fresh asparagus, cut in
   pieces (about 2½ cups)
1 cup light cream
2 tablespoons butter or margarine
  Butter or margarine

Heat water and salt to boiling. Add asparagus; cover and simmer till asparagus is tender, about 8 to 10 minutes. Put asparagus and cooking water in blender container; blend till asparagus is finely chopped. Add cream to mixture in blender container; blend smooth. Return soup to saucepan; add the 2 tablespoons butter and heat through. Dot each serving with butter or margarine. Serves 4.

EASY GREEN PEA SOUP

Puree canned peas in canned chicken broth mixture to make this easy soup—

1 13¾-ounce can chicken broth
1 cup milk
1 16-ounce can peas, drained
½ small onion
2 tablespoons butter or margarine
3 tablespoons all-purpose flour
⅛ teaspoon dried rosemary leaves,
   crushed
  Salt
  Pepper
4 slices bacon, crisp-cooked and
   crumbled

Put chicken broth, milk, peas, onion, butter or margarine, flour, and crushed rosemary in blender container; blend till peas are pureed. Pour soup into saucepan; cook and stir till mixture is thickened and bubbly. Season to taste with salt and pepper. Top each serving with crumbled bacon. Makes 4 servings.

BEAN SOUP

1 pound dry navy beans (2 cups)
3 medium carrots, sliced
2 quarts water
1 meaty ham bone (1¼ pounds)
2 teaspoons salt
¼ teaspoon pepper
1 bay leaf
1 medium onion, cut in pieces

Put about ⅓ of the dry navy beans in blender container; blend till beans are chopped. Transfer chopped beans to large kettle or Dutch oven. Repeat with remaining beans.

Put carrots in blender container; cover with *cold* water. Blend till coarsely chopped. Drain. Add chopped carrots, water, ham bone, salt, pepper, bay leaf, and onion to beans in large kettle. Cover; simmer mixture for 3 hours.

Remove ham bone and bay leaf from mixture. Add ⅓ of the bean mixture to blender at a time; blend till nearly smooth. Cut ham off bone; add ham to soup. Serves 8 to 10.

Blender tip: Blend ingredients for making sauces first and then cook. If your blender has measuring gradations, measure liquid directly in blender container. Add remaining sauce ingredients and blend till smooth. Cook according to the recipe directions.

CREAMY LENTIL SOUP

        1 large onion, cut in pieces
        1 cup lentils
    2½ cups water
        2 teaspoons salt
    ¼ teaspoon pepper
        1 clove garlic, minced
    ¼ cup tomato sauce
        1 bay leaf
    1½ cups milk

Blend onion in blender container till finely chopped. Rinse lentils; drain. Place in saucepan. Add onion and next 6 ingredients. Cover and simmer 1 hour. Remove bay leaf. Blend mixture in blender container till pureed; return to saucepan. Add milk; heat and stir till hot and blended. Season to taste. Serves 5 to 6.

BLENDER WHITE SAUCE

Use thin sauce for soups; medium sauce for sauces and creamed dishes or vegetables; and thick sauce for croquettes and soufflés—

Thin:
        1 cup milk
        1 tablespoon all-purpose flour
    ¼ teaspoon salt
        1 tablespoon butter or margarine
Medium:
        1 cup milk
        2 tablespoons all-purpose flour
    ¼ teaspoon salt
        2 tablespoons butter or margarine
Thick:
        1 cup milk
    ¼ cup all-purpose flour
    ¼ teaspoon salt
        3 tablespoons butter or margarine

Put milk, all-purpose flour, salt, and butter or margarine in blender container; blend till mixture is smooth. Pour sauce into saucepan. Cook quickly, stirring constantly, till mixture thickens and bubbles. Makes about 1 cup.

BREAD SAUCE

Keep sauce heated over a sauce warmer—

        1 cup hot milk
        2 tablespoons butter or margarine
    ¼ teaspoon salt
        White bread, crusts removed*

Warm blender container by filling with hot water and letting stand a minute or two; empty water. Put hot milk, butter or margarine, and salt in blender container; blend till ingredients are mixed. With blender running, break bread into pieces and add to blender container. Stop blender occasionally to check sauce consistency. Serve at once. Makes 1¼ cups.

*Use 3 to 4 slices of bread for thin sauce, 6 to 7 slices of bread for medium sauce, and 9 to 10 slices of bread for thick sauce. Unless a white-colored sauce is desired, leave the bread crusts on and use less bread.

BLENDER HOLLANDAISE

    3 egg yolks
    2 tablespoon lemon juice
    ½ teaspoon prepared mustard
       Dash cayenne
    ½ cup butter or margarine

Put egg yolks, lemon juice, prepared mustard, and dash cayenne in blender container; blend till ingredients are combined. Heat butter or margarine in saucepan till melted and almost boiling. With blender slowly running, slowly pour about a third of the hot butter, in a thin stream, into the blender container.

Turn blender to high speed; slowly pour in remaining hot butter, blending till mixture is smooth and thickened. Makes about 1 cup.

BLENDER GRAVY

    3 tablespoons meat fat drippings
    2 cups liquid
    ¼ cup all-purpose flour
       Salt
       Pepper
       Dash dried thyme leaves, crushed
       Few drops Kitchen Bouquet

Remove meat to hot platter. Leaving crusty bits of meat in pan, pour meat juices and fat into large measuring cup. Skim off fat, reserving 3 tablespoons. Add water, milk, or giblet broth to the meat juices to equal 2 cups. Combine fat, the 2 cups liquid, and flour in blender container; blend till mixture is smooth.

Return blended gravy to pan. Cook mixture quickly, stirring constantly, till gravy is thickened and bubbly. Season gravy to taste with salt and pepper. If desired, add a dash of dried thyme leaves, crushed, and a few drops Kitchen Bouquet. Makes about 2½ cups.

Smooth, versatile sauce

Enhance the flavor of garden-fresh vegetables, meat entrees, or elegant egg dishes with easy-to-make Blender Hollandaise.

TANGY BLUE CHEESE SAUCE

      1 cup dairy sour cream
      1 ounce blue cheese, crumbled (¼ cup)
      3 tablespoons milk
      1 green onion with top, sliced
      ¼ teaspoon salt
         Dash bottled hot pepper sauce

Put ingredients in blender; blend till onion is finely chopped. Heat through but do not boil. Serve over vegetables. Makes 1¼ cups. Note: Refrigerate and reheat unused sauce.

CUMBERLAND SAUCE

      1 1-inch square piece orange peel
      ¾ cup orange juice
      ½ cup currant jelly
      2 tablespoons claret
      ¼ teaspoon ground ginger
      4 teaspoons cornstarch
      1 tablespoon lemon juice

Put all ingredients in blender container. Blend till ingredients are combined and orange peel is finely chopped. Pour into saucepan; cook and stir till mixture is thickened and bubbly. Cook 1 to 2 minutes longer. Serve sauce hot or cold with meat or poultry. Makes 1½ cups.

SPANISH TOMATO SAUCE

      1 tablespoon butter or margarine
      ¼ small onion
      ¼ small green pepper
      ½ clove garlic
      1 16-ounce can tomatoes, undrained
      1 6-ounce can tomato paste
      1 teaspoon sugar
      ½ teaspoon dried oregano leaves, crushed
      ½ teaspoon pepper
         Dash salt

Put ingredients in blender container; blend till onion and green pepper are finely chopped. Simmer, covered, in saucepan for 30 minutes. Serve over meat or fish. Makes 3 cups.

TARTAR SAUCE

      1 cup mayonnaise or salad dressing
      1 tablespoon lemon juice
      1 large dill pickle, cut in pieces
      ¼ small onion
      1 hard-cooked egg, quartered
      1 tablespoon capers, drained
      1 teaspoon snipped chives

Put ingredients in blender container; blend till chopped. Chill. Serve with fish. Makes 2 cups.

BLENDER BÉARNAISE

      2 egg yolks
      1 tablespoon lemon juice
      1 teaspoon tarragon vinegar
      1 teaspoon fresh tarragon leaves, *or* dried tarragon leaves, crushed
      1 tablespoon capers, drained
      ¾ cup hot melted butter or margarine
      2 tablespoons snipped parsley

Blend first 5 ingredients in blender container. With blender running at low speed, gradually add a third of the butter in slow, steady stream. Turn blender to high speed; slowly add remaining butter. Fold in parsley. Serve with meat, fish, or poultry. Makes ¾ cup.

BLENDER SWEET-SOUR SAUCE

      1 6-ounce can frozen pineapple juice concentrate
      ½ cup brown sugar
      ¼ cup vinegar
      ¼ cup water
      ¼ small green pepper
      1 slice canned pimiento
      1 tablespoon cornstarch
      ½ teaspoon salt

Put all ingredients in blender container; blend till pimiento slice and green pepper are finely chopped. Cook and stir mixture till thickened and bubbly; cook 1 minute more. Use as a basting sauce for meat in last few minutes of broiling or roasting. Makes 1¼ cups.

MINUTE-TRIMMED MAIN DISHES

Keep your blender handy when preparing the main course for the meal. Many dishes depend on small bits of apple, celery, onion, or green pepper that can be chopped in the blender. These add a special flavor or seasoning touch to meat loaves, meatballs, skillet dishes, casseroles, or tasty stuffings.

Use your blender, too, to prepare cheeses, from cottage or cream to Swiss and Cheddar, in ways that complement a variety of meat and egg dishes and play a starring role in a classic fondue. All these favorites are twice as easy to prepare with a blender.

CHEESE-SAUCED MEAT LOAF

- ¾ cup milk
- 2 eggs
- 2 slices bread, torn in pieces
- ¼ small onion
- 1 teaspoon salt
- ½ teaspoon ground sage
  - Dash pepper
- 2 pounds ground beef
- 1 cup milk
- 2 tablespoons butter or margarine
- 2 tablespoons all-purpose flour
- 4 ounces sharp process American cheese, cut in cubes (1 cup)
- ½ slice canned pimiento

Place ¾ cup milk, eggs, bread, onion, salt, sage, and pepper in blender container. Blend till combined; add to ground beef in large mixing bowl. Mix well. Pat meat into a 9x5x3-inch loaf pan. Bake at 350° for 1½ hours.

Prepare cheese sauce by placing remaining ingredients in blender container. Blend till ingredients are combined and cheese is finely chopped. Transfer to saucepan. Cook and stir over low heat until sauce is thick and smooth. Place meat loaf on a serving platter. Spoon cheese sauce over top. Makes 8 servings.

MENU

Cheese-Sauced Meat Loaf*
Brussels Sprouts
Hard Rolls   **Butter**
Trifle*
Beverage

*See index listing for page number.

POT ROAST STROGANOFF

- 2- to 2½-pound beef chuck roast
- 3 tablespoons salad oil
- 1 10¾-ounce can condensed tomato soup
- 1 cup cream-style cottage cheese
- 1 tablespoon Worcestershire sauce
- ½ small onion, cut in pieces
- 1 clove garlic
- 1 3-ounce can mushrooms, drained
- 3 tablespoons all-purpose flour
- ⅛ cup water
  - Hot cooked noodles

Trim meat; season. Brown in oil in Dutch oven. Put next 5 ingredients in blender; blend smooth. Add mushrooms; pour over meat. Cover; cook at 325° about 2 hours. Place meat on platter. Skim fat from sauce. Combine flour and water; add to sauce. Cook and stir till thick; season. Serve on noodles. Serves 6.

Meat loaf favorite

Set the table with a British theme and →
serve tasty Cheese-Sauced Meat Loaf and surround it with bright Brussels sprouts.

STUFFED BEEF ROUNDS

Mellow cheese flavors the stuffing—

2 pounds beef round steak, ½
    inch thick
4 ounces sharp process American
    cheese, cut in cubes (1 cup)
½ slice bread
½ medium onion, cut in pieces
3 stalks celery, sliced
3 sprigs parsley
¼ cup all-purpose flour
1 teaspoon salt
⅛ teaspoon pepper
2 tablespoons salad oil
1 10½-ounce can condensed beef broth
½ teaspoon dry mustard
1 tablespoon all-purpose flour
¼ cup water

Cut steak into 6 pieces; pound to ¼-inch thickness. Place cheese and bread in blender container; blend till cheese is coarsely chopped. Remove from blender to bowl. Place onion, celery, and parsley in blender; blend till coarsely chopped. Add to cheese.

Divide the stuffing mixture among pieces of steak. Roll up each steak jelly-roll fashion; secure with wooden picks or tie with string. Combine the ¼ cup flour, the salt, and pepper. Roll meat in flour mixture to coat. In 10-inch skillet, slowly brown meat in hot oil. Drain off excess fat. Combine beef broth and dry mustard; pour over steak rolls. Cover and cook over low heat till meat is tender, about 1 to 1¼ hours. Remove meat to platter.

Skim excess fat from pan juices. Combine the 1 tablespoon flour and the water; stir into pan juices. Cook and stir till sauce thickens and bubbles; pour over meat. Serves 6.

Chop a delectable stuffing of cheese and vegetables in the blender for the Stuffed Beef Rounds entrée. The sauce is made with beef broth and mustard.

THREE-CHEESEBURGER BAKE

- 2 ounces sharp process cheese, cubed
- 1 slice bread, torn in pieces
- 2 pounds ground beef
- 1 15-ounce can tomato sauce
- ½ small onion, cut in pieces
- 1 teaspoon sugar
- 1 teaspoon salt
- ⅛ teaspoon garlic salt
- 1 cup packaged precooked rice
- ⅓ cup milk
- 1 cup cream-style cottage cheese
- 1 3-ounce package cream cheese, cubed
- ½ small green pepper, cut in pieces

Put cheese and bread in blender. Blend till chopped; reserve. In skillet brown beef; pour off fat. Put next 5 ingredients in blender; blend till onion is chopped. Add to beef. Add rice. Put next 3 ingredients in blender; blend smooth. Add pepper; blend till chopped. Put *half* of meat in an 8x8x2-inch baking dish. Pour cheese mixture over. Top with meat. Cover; bake at 350° for 35 to 40 minutes. Uncover; top with cheese and crumbs. Bake to melt cheese. Serves 6 to 8.

HAWAIIAN BEEF LOAVES

- 1 envelope brown gravy mix
- ½ cup milk
- 1 thin slice of onion
- 2 eggs
- 1 sprig parsley
- 2 teaspoons soy sauce
- ½ teaspoon salt
- 1½ slices bread, torn in pieces
- 2 pounds ground beef
- 1 8¾-ounce can apricot halves
- ¼ cup vinegar
- ⅓ cup brown sugar

Put first 9 ingredients in blender; blend to mix. Combine with beef; shape two loaves. Bake in shallow pan at 350° for 50 minutes. Put remaining ingredients in blender; blend smooth. Simmer 5 minutes. Glaze meat with sauce. Bake 15 minutes. Pass sauce with meat. Makes 8 servings.

MEXICAN BEEF TOSTADAS

Featured in the photograph on page 4—

- 1 small onion, cut in pieces
- 1 clove garlic, halved
- 1 pound ground beef
- ½ teaspoon salt
- ½ teaspoon chili powder
- 8 ounces sharp process American cheese, cut in cubes (2 cups)
- ½ slice bread, torn in pieces
- 1 small head lettuce, cut in eighths
- 2 medium tomatoes, quartered
- 12 tortillas (canned or frozen)
  Salad oil
  Mexican Fried Beans (*see page 38*)
  Hot Sauce for Tostadas

Put onion and garlic in blender container; blend till coarsely chopped. In skillet cook beef, onion, and garlic till meat is browned. Drain off fat. Add salt and chili powder.

Place cheese and bread in blender container; blend till coarsely chopped. Transfer to small bowl. Place lettuce in blender; cover with cold water. Blend till coarsely chopped. Drain well. Transfer to small bowl. Place tomatoes in blender container; blend till coarsely chopped. Drain well. Transfer to small bowl.

In skillet fry tortillas till crisp in ¼ inch hot oil. Drain. Spoon about ¼ cup meat mixture onto each. Top with Mexican Fried Beans, tomato, lettuce, and cheese. Pass Hot Sauce for Tostadas.

HOT SAUCE FOR TOSTADAS

- 1 16-ounce can tomatoes
- 1 tablespoon salad oil
- 1 small onion, cut in pieces
- ½ teaspoon dried oregano, crushed
- 1 tablespoon wine vinegar
- 1 4-ounce can green chilies, drained

Drain tomatoes, reserving 2 tablespoons juice. Put tomatoes, reserved juice, oil, onion, oregano, vinegar, and *one* of the chilies in blender. Blend almost smooth. Add more chilies, if desired. Blend smooth. Makes 2¼ cups.

HAM BALLS IN BERRY SAUCE

> 3 cups cubed, fully cooked ham
> 3 slices bread, torn in pieces
> 2 eggs
> ¼ cup milk
> 2 tablespoons shortening or salad oil
> 1 8-ounce can jellied cranberry sauce
> 1 tablespoon bottled steak sauce
> 1½ teaspoons brown sugar
> 1½ teaspoons salad oil
> 1 teaspoon prepared mustard

Place ½ *cup* ham in blender; blend till coarsely chopped. Set aside. Repeat. Put bread, eggs, and milk in blender; blend to combine. Mix with ham; shape into 18 balls. Brown balls in hot oil. Drain. Place remaining ingredients in blender; blend smooth. Pour over balls. Cover; cook 20 minutes. Serves 6.

Prepare a different holiday dinner, featuring Apple-Kraut Pork Roast. Herbed apple stuffing bakes in specially cut pockets.

APPLE-KRAUT PORK ROAST

> 3 stalks celery, sliced
> ½ medium onion, cut in pieces
> 6 tablespoons butter or margarine
> 3 medium apples, peeled, cut in eighths, and cored
> 1 8-ounce can sauerkraut, undrained
> 3 cups croutons
> ½ teaspoons salt
> ½ teaspoon ground sage
> 4- to 4½-pound pork rib roast, backbone loosened, pockets cut between ribs

Put celery and onion in blender; add cold water to cover. Blend till coarsely chopped; drain. Cook in butter till tender but not brown. Put apple and kraut in blender; blend till chopped. Combine remaining ingredients, except pork. Stuff ⅓ cup mixture into each pocket of roast. Insert meat thermometer in center of meat. Roast, fat side up, in open roasting pan at 325° till thermometer registers 170°, 2 hours. Bake extra stuffing in 1-quart covered casserole last ½ hour. Serves 8.

RIBS WITH MOCK MINCEMEAT

> 6 pounds pork spareribs
> 1½ cups water
> Salt
> 1 beef bouillon cube
> ½ cup hot water
> 1 medium apple, peeled, cut in eighths, and cored
> 1 cup raisins
> ½ cup jellied cranberry sauce
> ¼ cup lemon juice
> 1 teaspoon grated orange peel
> ½ teaspoon ground cinnamon
> ¼ teaspoon ground cloves
> ¼ teaspoon ground ginger

Cut ribs in serving-sized pieces; place, meat side up, in roasting pan. Add water; season. Cover with foil. Bake at 350° for 1½ hours. In blender dissolve bouillon in hot water. Add remaining ingredients; blend to chop apple. Drain ribs; top with mincemeat. Bake, uncovered, 30 to 45 minutes. Serves 6 to 8.

Blender tip: Make crumbs for meat loaf or meatballs, and combine milk, eggs, and seasonings in one blending operation. Mix the blended mixture with ground meat.

SAUSAGE SKILLET SUPPER

　1　small onion, cut in pieces
½　medium green pepper, cut in pieces
　1　pound bulk pork sausage
　1　16-ounce can tomatoes,
　　　undrained and cut up
　1　cup uncooked elbow macaroni
½　cup tomato juice *or* water
　1　tablespoon sugar
　1　teaspoon salt
½　teaspoon chili powder
　1　cup dairy sour cream

Place onion and green pepper in blender container; blend till coarsely chopped. Cook sausage, onion, and pepper till meat browns; break up sausage as it cooks. Drain off fat. Add remaining ingredients, except sour cream. Cover. Simmer 20 minutes; stir often. Add sour cream. Heat; do not boil. Serves 4 or 5.

SPICY CHOPS AND CABBAGE

　4　pork loin chops, ¾ inch thick
　2　tablespoons water
½　teaspoon salt
　2　whole cloves
½　small bay leaf
　1　medium head cabbage, cored and
　　　cut in small wedges
　3　medium apples, peeled, cut in
　　　eighths, and cored
½　small onion, cut in pieces
¼　cup sugar
1½　teaspoons all-purpose flour
½　teaspoon salt
　2　tablespoons vinegar
　2　tablespoons water

Trim fat from meat; cook fat in skillet to oil surface. Discard trimmings. Brown chops in skillet. Add next 4 ingredients. Cover; simmer 30 minutes. Remove chops from skillet. Discard cloves and bay leaf. Fill blender container with cabbage; add cold water to cover. Blend till coarsely chopped. Drain well. Add to skillet; repeat. Put ⅓ of apple pieces and onion in blender; add cold water to cover. Blend till coarsely chopped. Add to cabbage; repeat. Put remaining ingredients in blender; blend to mix. Pour over cabbage; stir to mix. Cover; simmer 5 minutes. Return chops to skillet; cover. Cook 20 minutes. Serves 4.

CRAB NEWBURG

1¾　cups milk
¼　cup butter or margarine
　3　egg yolks
　2　tablespoons all-purpose flour
½　teaspoon salt
¼　teaspoon paprika
　1　7½-ounce can crab meat, drained,
　　　flaked, and cartilage removed
　4　patty shells

Put first 6 ingredients in blender container; blend till smooth. Pour into saucepan; cook over medium heat, stirring constantly, till mixture thickens and bubbles. Add crab; heat through. Serve in patty shells. Serves 4.

OMELET PARMENTIER

　1　large potato, peeled and
　　　cut in pieces
　1　tablespoon snipped chives
　¼　teaspoon salt
　2　tablespoons butter or margarine
　4　eggs
　⅛　teaspoon salt

Put potato in blender; add *cold* water to cover. Blend till coarsely chopped; drain. In covered 8-inch skillet cook potato, chives, and ¼ teaspoon salt in butter over medium-low heat for 10 minutes. Put eggs and ⅛ teaspoon salt in blender; blend to combine. Pour eggs onto potato mixture; cook over low heat, stirring lightly through top of uncooked egg, till almost set. Cover; cook till surface of omelet is set but shiny, about 3 minutes. Serves 4.

Pop big chicken pieces coated with crunchy herb-cheese-crumb mixture into the oven to prepare easy Crispy Parmesan Chicken.

STUFFED CORNISH HENS

　6　slices dry bread
　½　small onion
　2　stalks celery, sliced
　¼　cup butter or margarine
　2　medium oranges
　½　teaspoon poultry seasoning
　½　teaspoon salt
　　　Dash pepper
　4　1-pound ready-to-cook Cornish
　　　game hens
　　　Butter or margarine, melted

Break bread into blender container; blend to make coarse crumbs. Transfer to large bowl. Put onion and celery in blender; add *cold* water to cover. Blend till coarsely chopped. Drain. Cook vegetables in the ¼ cup butter till tender but not brown.

Peel oranges, reserving 1-inch square piece of orange peel. Quarter oranges, removing seeds; add orange pieces to blender with peel, poultry seasoning, ½ teaspoon salt, and pepper. Blend till orange is coarsely chopped.

Toss celery, onion, and orange mixture with crumbs. Season hens inside and out with salt. Lightly stuff birds; place, breast side up, on rack in shallow pan. Brush with butter. Roast, covered, at 400° for 30 minutes. Uncover; roast till drumstick moves easily, about 1 hour. Brush birds with melted butter during last 15 minutes. Serves 4.

CRISPY PARMESAN CHICKEN

　1½　cups croutons
　¾　cup grated Parmesan cheese
　2　sprigs parsley
　1　2½- to 3-pound ready-to-cook
　　　broiler-fryer chicken, cut up
　½　cup butter or margarine, melted

Put croutons, cheese, and parsley in blender. Blend till croutons are fine crumbs. Dip chicken in butter; roll in crumb mixture. Place pieces, skin side up, in shallow baking pan. Sprinkle with remaining butter and crumbs. Bake, without turning, at 375° till tender, about 45 minutes to 1 hour. Makes 4 servings.

MENU

Stuffed Cornish Hens*
Cumberland Sauce*
Chinese Pea Pods
Hot Rolls   Butter
Three-Fruit Sherbet*
Beverage

*See index listing for page number.

POTATO-STUFFED CHICKEN

1 large apple, peeled, cut in eighths, and cored
½ medium onion, cut in pieces
6 tablespoons butter or margarine
2½ slices soft bread, torn in pieces
1 17-ounce can vacuum-packed sweet potatoes, drained
1 tablespoon sugar
1 teaspoon salt
¼ teaspoon ground nutmeg
• • •
2 2-pound ready-to-cook broiler-fryer chickens
Salt
Salad oil

Put apple and onion in blender; blend till coarsely chopped. Cook in butter till tender. Put bread in blender; blend to coarse crumbs. Transfer to mixing bowl. Put sweet potatoes, sugar, salt, and nutmeg in blender; blend till potatoes are smooth. Combine cooked apple and onion, crumbs, and potato mixture; mix.

Rinse birds; pat dry. Lightly salt insides. Stuff with potato mixture. Truss and place, breast side up, on racks in shallow roasting pans. Rub skins with oil. Insert meat thermometer into center of inside of thigh muscle, making sure bulb does not touch bone.

Roast, uncovered, at 375° for 1 hour. Brush dry areas of skin occasionally with pan drippings. Cut band of skin or string between legs and tail. Continue roasting till meat thermometer registers 185°, 15 to 30 minutes.

MACARONI PUFF SOUFFLÉ

½ cup elbow macaroni, cooked
1 3-ounce can mushrooms, drained
1 cup milk
3 egg yolks
½ small onion, cut in pieces
3 tablespoons all-purpose flour
½ teaspoon salt
¼ small green pepper, cut in pieces
4 ounces sharp process American cheese, cut in cubes (1 cup)
3 egg whites
¼ teaspoon cream of tartar

Put macaroni and enough water to cover in blender; blend to coarsely chop. Drain; pour into saucepan. Add mushrooms. Put next 5 ingredients in blender; blend till smooth. Add green pepper and cheese; blend till coarsely chopped. Pour over macaroni. Cook and stir till mixture thickens. Beat egg whites with cream of tartar to stiff peaks. Fold into macaroni. Bake in ungreased 1½-quart soufflé dish at 325° for 50 to 55 minutes. Serves 6.

BLENDER CHEESE FONDUE

8 ounces Gruyère cheese, cut in cubes (2 cups)
2 cups dry white wine
16 ounces natural Swiss cheese, cut in cubes (4 cups)
1½ tablespoons all-purpose flour
1 teaspoon ground nutmeg
1 teaspoon pepper
1 clove garlic
French bread, cut in bite-sized pieces, each with one crust

Put Gruyère cheese in blender; blend till finely chopped; set aside. Warm the wine. Put *2 cups* of Swiss cheese in blender with flour, nutmeg, pepper, and garlic; blend till finely chopped. With blender at low speed gradually add warm wine, then Swiss cheese; blend smooth. Pour into saucepan. Add Gruyère. Cook and stir over low heat till thick. Pour into fondue pot; keep warm. Spear bread on forks; dip in cheese. Serves 10.

HURRY-UP VEGETABLES

Presenting cooked vegetables in new and interesting guises need not stump you when you have a blender to lend assistance. Plan tempting meals around beets, broccoli, Brussels sprouts, carrots, cabbage, lima beans, potatoes, and squash, all cut up or pureed efficiently in your blender container.

Crusty fritters and brightly seasoned casseroles head the list of family pleasers, but many favorites from around the world adapt to the blender, also. These include vegetables served tempura-style as enjoyed in Japan, hearty potato pancakes of German origin, plus a delicious version of fried beans to accompany a number of Mexican specialties.

MEXICAN FRIED BEANS

Use these beans as part of the Mexican Beef Tostada filling as shown on page 4—

> 6 slices bacon
> 2 15-ounce cans kidney beans
> ½ teaspoon salt

In a 10-inch skillet cook the bacon slices till they are crisp. Drain the bacon, reserving 2 tablespoons of the bacon drippings.

Put *1 can* of the kidney beans *with liquid* in blender container. Put ½ teaspoon salt, crisp-cooked bacon, and the 2 tablespoons reserved bacon drippings in blender container. Adjust lid; blend till ingredients are thoroughly combined. (When necessary, stop blender and use rubber spatula to scrape down sides.

Return bean mixture to skillet. Drain remaining can of kidney beans; stir beans into blended mixture in skillet, mashing slightly. Cook bean mixture, uncovered, over low heat, stirring frequently till mixture is thickened, about 10 minutes. Makes 4 to 6 servings.
Special cooking tip: Be sure to refrigerate or freeze any leftover fried beans. When heated another day in hot oil or shortening, this Mexican favorite becomes Refried Beans.

CHEESY BROCCOLI FRITTERS

> 1 cup milk
> 1 egg
> 2 cups sifted all-purpose flour
> 2 teaspoons baking powder
> ¾ teaspoon salt
> 1½ cups fresh broccoli, cut in 1-inch
>   pieces
>   Fat for frying
> 1 cup milk
> 2 ounces process American cheese, cut
>   in cubes (½ cup)
> 2 ounces process Swiss cheese, cut in
>   cubes (½ cup)
> 2 tablespoons all-purpose flour
> 2 tablespoons butter, softened

Put 1 cup milk, egg, 2 cups flour, baking powder, salt, and broccoli in blender container. Blend till broccoli is finely chopped. (When necessary, stop blender and use rubber spatula to scrape down sides of container.) Drop mixture from tablespoon into deep hot fat (375°). Fry, a few at a time, till golden brown, about 3 to 4 minutes. Drain on paper toweling.

Put 1 cup milk, American cheese, Swiss cheese, 2 tablespoons flour, and softened butter in blender container; blend till ingredients are combined. In saucepan cook and stir mixture over low heat till thickened and bubbly. Serve cheese sauce atop fritters. Makes 24.

LIMA BEAN BAKE

A peppy tomato sauce complements the lima beans topped with crisp-cooked bacon—

- 1 8-ounce can tomato sauce
- ½ medium onion, cut in pieces
- ¼ cup brown sugar
- 1 tablespoon prepared mustard
- ½ teaspoon salt
  Dash pepper
  Dash Worcestershire sauce
- 3 15-ounce cans dried lima beans, drained
- 4 slices bacon, crisp-cooked and crumbled

Put tomato sauce, onion pieces, brown sugar, prepared mustard, ½ teaspoon salt, dash pepper, and dash Worcestershire sauce in blender container. Adjust lid on the blender container; blend till the onion is finely chopped and all of the ingredients are thoroughly combined.

Combine tomato sauce mixture with the drained dried lima beans. Pour the bean mixture into a 1½-quart casserole; top with crisp-cooked and crumbled bacon. Bake mixture, uncovered, at 375° for 1 hour. Serves 8.

Special serving hint: Tote this barbecue-flavored pot of beans along to your next outdoor get-together. Or serve it to Dad and those hungry youngsters who have been out sledding in the cold winter snow all morning.

Spoon creamy cheese sauce over crisp Cheesy Broccoli Fritters just before serving. Delicate cheese flavor enhances tender, fresh, broccoli-flavored fritters.

ORANGY BEETS

  1½ pounds fresh beets
   2 medium oranges
   3 tablespoons brown sugar
   1 tablespoon cornstarch
  ¼ teaspoon salt
      Dash pepper
   2 tablespoons butter or margarine

Cut off all but 1-inch of the beet stem and root. Wash and scrub thoroughly; do not peel. Cook beets, covered, in boiling, salted water till tender, about 35 to 40 minutes for medium-sized beets. Drain, reserving ⅓ cup of the cooking liquid. Peel beets; cut in 1-inch pieces.

Peel and quarter oranges, discarding seeds. Put orange in blender container; blend till pureed. Add brown sugar, cornstarch, salt, pepper, and *half* of the beets to orange in blender container; turn on and off quickly till beets are coarsely chopped. Pour into saucepan. Repeat with reserved cooking liquid and remaining beets. Add to saucepan along with butter. Cook and stir till thickened and bubbly; cook 2 minutes longer. Serves 6.

BROCCOLI BAKE

   2 10-ounce packages frozen chopped
      broccoli
   1 slice bread, torn in pieces
  ¾ cup milk
   4 ounces process American cheese,
      cut in cubes (1 cup)
   2 tablespoons all-purpose flour
  ½ teaspoon salt
   2 hard-cooked eggs, coarsely chopped
   2 tablespoons butter or margarine,
      melted

Prepare frozen broccoli according to package directions; drain. Put bread in blender container; blend till bread is in coarse crumbs. Set aside crumbs. Put milk, cheese, flour, and salt in blender container. Blend till mixture is smooth; combine with broccoli and eggs. Pour into 1-quart casserole. Combine butter and crumbs; sprinkle atop casserole. Bake at 350° for 35 to 40 minutes. Serves 4 to 6.

BRUSSELS SPROUTS SUPREME

   2 10-ounce packages frozen Brussels
      sprouts
  1¼ cups milk
   2 tablespoons butter or margarine
   2 tablespoons all-purpose flour
  ¼ teaspoon salt
   2 ounces sharp natural Cheddar cheese,
      cut in cubes (½ cup)
   1 5-ounce can water chestnuts,
      drained

Cook Brussels sprouts according to package directions; drain. Cut any large Brussels sprouts in half. Put milk, butter or margarine, flour, salt, and cubes of cheese in blender container; blend till mixture is smooth. Add water chestnuts; blend till coarsely chopped. Pour mixture into saucepan; cook and stir till thickened and bubbly. Stir in drained Brussels sprouts; heat through. Serves 6 to 8.

VEGETABLE TEMPURA

      Assorted fresh vegetables such as
      asparagus spears, parsley, sweet
      potatoes, spinach, mushrooms, and
      green beans
      Salad oil
   1 cup sifted all-purpose flour
   1 cup ice water
   1 slightly beaten egg
   2 tablespoons salad oil
  ½ teaspoon sugar
  ½ teaspoon salt
      Ice cubes
      Tempura Condiments

Wash and dry vegetables; cut any large pieces in strips. Fill skillet ½ full with oil; heat to 360° to 365°. Put flour, ice water, egg, salad oil, sugar, and salt in blender container; blend till combined. Pour into bowl; stir in one or two ice cubes. Dip vegetables in cold batter. Fry in hot oil till golden; drain.

Serve with Tempura Condiments: 1. grated fresh gingeroot; 2. equal parts grated turnip and radish, combined; and 3. ½ cup prepared mustard mixed with 3 tablespoons soy sauce.

Blender tip: Cut vegetables into ½ to 1-inch size pieces before putting in blender container. When chopping more than ½ cup, cover vegetables with *cold* water. Adjust lid; turn blender on and off quickly.

COMPANY CABBAGE

    2   tablespoons butter or margarine
    1   medium head cabbage, cut in wedges
    1   clove garlic, minced
    ½   cup dairy sour cream
    1   tablespoon sugar
    2   tablespoons vinegar
    1   teaspoon salt
    ¼   teaspoon caraway seed (optional)

Heat butter in skillet. Put *half* of cabbage in blender container; cover with *cold* water. Blend till coarsely chopped; drain, reserving ¼ cup water. Repeat process with remaining cabbage. Add cabbage, garlic, and the ¼ cup water to skillet; cover and steam over low heat 10 to 12 minutes. Combine sour cream, sugar, vinegar, and salt; stir into cabbage. Heat through; top with caraway seed. Serves 6.

RED CABBAGE DELUXE

    ½   small head red cabbage
    1   medium apple, unpeeled and cored
    1   small onion
    2   tablespoons butter or margarine
    1   tablespoon brown sugar
    ¼   cup vinegar
    1   teaspoon caraway seed
    ½   teaspoon salt
        Dash pepper

Cut cabbage into small wedges; remove core. Cut apple and onion in quarters. Fill blender container with *half* the vegetables; cover with *cold* water. Blend till vegetables are coarsely chopped; drain. Repeat.

  Melt butter or margarine in heavy skillet. Add chopped vegetables and the remaining ingredients to melted butter in skillet. Cover and cook over low heat, stirring occasionally, till vegetables are almost tender, about 10 minutes. Uncover; cook and stir till cabbage is tender, about 1 to 2 minutes. Serves 6.

SPANISH CORN SCALLOP

    25 rich round cheese crackers
    ¾   cup milk
    1   egg
    ½   medium green pepper, cut in pieces
    1   2-ounce can sliced pimiento,
          drained
    ¼   teaspoon salt
    1   17-ounce can cream-style corn
    2   tablespoons butter or margarine,
          melted

Put *half* the crackers in blender container; blend to coarse crumbs. Repeat with remaining crackers; remove crumbs and set aside.

  Put milk, egg, green pepper, pimiento, and salt in blender container; blend till green pepper is coarsely chopped. Measure ½ cup crumbs; reserve. Combine remaining crumbs with vegetable mixture and cream-style corn. Pour mixture into 8-inch round baking dish. Combine ½ cup reserved crumbs with melted butter or margarine; sprinkle over corn mixture. Bake at 350° for 35 minutes. Serves 6.

POTATO PANCAKES

    2 eggs
    ¼ cup milk
    ½ small onion, cut in pieces
    ¼ cup all-purpose flour
    ¼ teaspoon baking powder
    1 teaspoon salt
      Dash pepper
    4 medium potatoes, peeled and cut in
      pieces
      Fresh Applesauce (*see page 63*)

Put first 7 ingredients and *half* the potatoes in blender container; blend till potatoes are coarsely chopped. Add remaining potatoes; blend till coarsely chopped. Bake on medium-hot, lightly greased griddle, using ¼ cup batter for each pancake. (Use a spatula to spread batter evenly.) Brown one side; turn. Brown other side, about 2 to 3 minutes more. Serve with Fresh Applesauce. Makes 12 pancakes.

After baking, place cheese triangles atop easy Hash Brown Scallop of frozen hash brown potatoes and fresh carrots.

HASH BROWN SCALLOP

    4 slices sharp process American
      cheese
    1 slice bread, torn in pieces
    2 chicken bouillon cubes
    1 cup hot water
    1 medium carrot, sliced
    2 green onions with tops, sliced
    4 cups frozen loose-pack hash brown
      potatoes, thawed (16 ounces)
      Dash pepper
    1 tablespoon butter or margarine

Cut *1 slice* cheese into 2 triangles; reserve. Break up remaining cheese and put in blender container with bread; blend till cheese is coarsely chopped. Remove and set aside.

Put bouillon cubes and hot water in blender container; blend till cubes are dissolved. Add carrot and green onion to mixture in blender container; blend till coarsely chopped.

Combine carrot mixture, chopped cheese, hash brown potatoes, and pepper. Turn into 1½-quart casserole. Dot with butter or margarine. Bake, covered, at 375° till potatoes are tender, about 40 minutes, stirring occasionally. Top with reserved cheese. Bake till cheese melts, 1 to 2 minutes. Serves 6.

POTATO-CHEESE CUSTARD

    1 cup milk
    3 eggs
    1 5-ounce jar process cheese spread
      with bacon
    ¼ small onion
    1 large sprig parsley
    ½ teaspoon salt
    ½ teaspoon dry mustard
    3 medium potatoes, peeled and cut
      in pieces

Put milk, eggs, cheese spread, onion, parsley, salt, and dry mustard in blender container; blend till combined. Add potato pieces, a few at a time; blend till potatoes are chopped. Turn mixture into ungreased 10x6x1¾-inch baking dish. Bake at 350° till potatoes are tender, about 50 to 55 minutes. Makes 6 servings.

CARROT-CHEDDAR BAKE

        6 medium carrots, sliced
     ½ teaspoon salt
     20 to 22 saltine crackers
    1½ cups milk
        2 eggs
        4 ounces natural Cheddar cheese, cut
             in cubes (1 cup)
        2 tablespoons butter or margarine
     ½ teaspoon salt

Put *half* the carrots and ½ teaspoon salt in blender container; cover with *cold* water. Blend till coarsely chopped. Transfer to saucepan. Repeat with remaining carrots. Bring to boiling; reduce heat. Cover and simmer till carrots are tender, 10 to 15 minutes. Drain.

Wipe blender container dry. Break a few crackers into container; blend to coarse crumbs. Remove and set aside. Repeat with remaining crackers. Put remaining ingredients in blender; blend till cheese is finely chopped.

Combine carrots, cracker crumbs, and cheese mixture. Turn into ungreased 8x1½-inch round baking dish. Bake at 350° till set, about 35 to 40 minutes. Makes 6 servings.

VEGETABLE-CHEESE MEDLEY

     ¼ cup peanuts (optional)
        2 medium carrots, sliced
        1 cup cold water
     ¼ cup milk
        1 3-ounce package cream cheese, cut
             in cubes and softened
        1 tablespoon all-purpose flour
        1 16-ounce can small whole onions,
             drained and cut in half

Put peanuts in blender container; blend till coarsely chopped. Remove and set aside. Put carrots and water in blender container; blend till coarsely chopped. Drain off ½ cup of the water. Cook carrots, covered, in remaining water till tender. Put milk, cream cheese, and flour in blender container; blend till mixture is smooth. Add cheese mixture to onions and carrots. Cook and stir over low heat till thickened and bubbly. Top with nuts. Serves 4.

STUFFED ZUCCHINI SQUASH

        3 medium zucchini squash (1½ pounds)
     24 saltine crackers
        1 egg
        2 ounces sharp natural Cheddar cheese,
             cut in cubes (½ cup)
        1 slice of small onion
     ½ slice canned pimiento
        2 sprigs parsley
     ½ teaspoon salt
             Dash pepper
        1 tablespoon melted butter or
             margarine

Wash zucchini; cut off ends. Cook in boiling, salted water for 5 minutes. Halve zucchini lengthwise; scoop out pulp and reserve. Put *half* of the crackers in blender container; blend to make coarse crumbs. Repeat with remaining crackers. Pour into bowl, reserving ¼ cup.

Place zucchini pulp, egg, cubes of cheese, onion, pimiento, parsley, salt, and pepper in blender container; blend till zucchini is coarsely chopped. Stir into crumbs. Fill zucchini shells with chopped mixture. Toss reserved crumbs with butter; sprinkle over top. Bake at 350° for 30 to 35 minutes. Makes 6 servings.

Fill Stuffed Zucchini Squash halves with colorful confetti combination of crackers, cheese, pimiento, parsley, and squash.

TIMESAVING BREADS

Using mixing techniques adapted for the blender, you can bake fragrant, homemade breads of both yeast-raised and quick-bread varieties. In each type the dry ingredients are incorporated in such a way that you get a light, tender product you'll be proud to serve. Cranberries, apricots, dates, oranges, nuts, cheeses, carrots, herbs, and spices contribute flavor to a delectable assortment of buns, loaves, muffins, pancakes, and waffles.

```
┌─────────────────────────────────┐
│           MENU                   │
│                                  │
│        Bean Soup*                │
│     Bacon-Onion Bread*           │
│     Assorted Crisp Relishes      │
│     Three-Fruit Sherbet*         │
│         Beverage                 │
│                                  │
│  *See index listing for page number. │
└─────────────────────────────────┘
```

BACON-ONION BREAD

2½ cups sifted all-purpose flour
1 package bacon-onion dip mix
1 package active dry yeast
¼ teaspoon baking soda
    • • •
1 cup cream-style cottage cheese
⅓ cup water
1 tablespoon butter or margarine
1 egg
   Butter
   Coarse salt (optional)

In blender container place *1 cup* of the flour, the dip mix, yeast, and baking soda. Switch blender on and off to combine. In saucepan heat together cottage cheese, water, and butter, stirring just till butter melts. Add to mixture in blender container along with egg. Blend at medium speed till thoroughly blended. (When necessary, stop blender and push batter from sides with rubber spatula.)

Pour the blended mixture into a large mixing bowl and, by hand, gradually stir in the remaining flour. Cover dough; let rise till double in bulk, about 1½ hours. Stir down. Shape into loaf and place in well-greased 8½x4½x 2½-inch loaf pan. Let rise till nearly double in bulk, about 40 minutes. Bake at 350° for 50 to 55 minutes. Cover loaf loosely with foil last 15 minutes to prevent overbrowning of the loaf. Remove from pans; brush with butter and sprinkle with coarse salt. Makes 1 loaf.

BLENDER WHITE BREAD

3¼ to 3½ cups sifted all-purpose flour
1 package active dry yeast
1 cup milk
¼ cup shortening
2 tablespoons sugar
1 teaspoon salt
1 egg

Place *1½ cups* of the flour and yeast in blender container. Switch on and off to combine. Heat milk, shortening, sugar, and salt just till warm, stirring till shortening is melted. Add to dry ingredients in blender. Add egg. Blend at low speed until combined. Blend at high speed till smooth, only 4 to 5 seconds.

Pour into mixing bowl. Stir in enough flour to make a moderately stiff dough. Cover and let rise till double, about 45 minutes. Punch down. Turn onto lightly floured surface; let rest 10 minutes. Shape loaf. Put in greased 9x5x3-inch loaf pan. Let rise until double. Bake at 375° for 40 to 45 minutes. Makes 1.

No kneading necessary

Bake hearty loaves of Bacon-Onion Bread → flavored with bacon-onion dip mix for those big, hungry appetites in your family.

BERRY-APPLE BUNS

Join bright cranberries with apples in a lightly spiced filling for these coffeetime favorites—

4¾ to 5¼ cups sifted all-purpose flour
2 packages active dry yeast
1⅛ cups milk
½ cup sugar
½ cup shortening
1¼ teaspoons salt
2 eggs
1½ cups fresh cranberries
2 small apples, cut in eighths and cored
¾ cup sugar
1½ teaspoons ground cinnamon
Sifted confectioners' sugar

Place *2 cups* of the flour and the 2 packages of yeast in blender container. Switch on and off to combine. In a small saucepan heat milk, sugar, shortening, and salt just till warm, stirring occasionally to melt shortening. Add to dry mixture in blender container. Add eggs. Adjust lid; blend at low speed until combined. (When necessary, stop blender and use rubber spatula to scrape down sides of container.) Continue blending at high speed just till batter is smooth, only 4 to 5 seconds.

Pour mixture into a large mixing bowl and stir in, by hand, enough of the remaining flour to make a soft dough. Cover and let rise till dough is double in bulk, about 1½ hours.

Punch down. Divide dough into 2 balls. Let rest 10 minutes. Divide each ball into 8 pieces and form each of these into a bun. Place buns about 2 inches apart on a greased baking sheet; flatten slightly. Cover and let rise till double. Make a slight indentation in the center of each bun, leaving ½ inch around edge of bun.

Put cranberries and apple pieces in blender container. Adjust lid; blend till fruits are coarsely chopped. Add sugar and ground cinnamon. Switch blender on and off once or twice to distribute sugar and spice.

Spoon filling into the indentations in the buns. Bake in a 400° oven till done, about 15 minutes. Remove from the baking sheet immediately and sprinkle tops of buns lightly with sifted confectioners' sugar. Makes 16.

ENGLISH MUFFINS

5¾ to 6 cups sifted all-purpose flour
2 packages active dry yeast
2 cups milk
2 tablespoons shortening
2 tablespoons sugar
2 teaspoons salt
Cornmeal

Place *2 cups* of the flour and dry yeast in blender container. Switch on and off to combine. Heat milk, shortening, sugar, and salt just till warm, stirring to melt shortening. Add to flour and yeast in blender container. Blend on low speed till smooth. Transfer batter to mixing bowl. By hand, stir in enough of remaining flour for a moderately stiff dough.

Turn onto lightly floured surface; knead till smooth, about 8 to 10 minutes. Place dough in greased bowl, turning once. Cover; let rise till double, about 1¼ hours. Punch down; cover and let rest 10 minutes. Roll to slightly less than ½ inch on surface sprinkled with cornmeal. Let rest 5 minutes. Cut with a 4-inch round cutter. Cover; let rise till very light, about 45 minutes. Bake on medium-hot, greased griddle, about 30 minutes, turning often. Cool. Split; toast both sides. Makes 24.

CRANBERRY-PECAN BREAD

3 cups sifted all-purpose flour
1 cup sugar
4 teaspoons baking powder
1 teaspoon salt
1½ cups milk
1 egg
2 tablespoons salad oil
1 cup fresh cranberries
½ cup pecans

Sift dry ingredients into mixing bowl; set aside. Place milk, egg, and oil in blender container; blend to combine. Add berries and nuts. Blend till cranberries are coarsely chopped. Pour blender mixture over dry ingredients; stir just to moisten. Turn batter into a greased 9x5x3-inch loaf pan. Bake at 350° about 1¼ hours. Remove from pan; cool on rack. Makes 1 loaf.

CHOCO-DATE NUT BREAD

2 cups sifted all-purpose flour
1 teaspoon baking soda
1 cup pitted dates
1 cup boiling water
2 1-ounce squares unsweetened
    chocolate, cut in pieces
½ cup walnuts
¼ cup shortening
1 egg
1 cup sugar
1 teaspoon vanilla
½ teaspoon salt

Into large mixing bowl sift together flour and baking soda; set aside. Place dates in blender container. Pour boiling water over dates; let cool to lukewarm. Add chocolate, walnuts, shortening, egg, sugar, vanilla, and salt to blender container. Blend till well mixed. Pour date mixture over dry ingredients. Stir just to moisten. Turn into greased and floured 9x5x3-inch loaf pan. Bake at 350° 1 hour. Cool 10 minutes. Remove from pan. Makes 1 loaf.

APRICOT-ALMOND BREAD

2 cups sifted all-purpose flour
1 cup sugar
1 tablespoon baking powder
½ teaspoon salt
¾ cup dried apricots
1 12-ounce can apricot nectar
½ cup almonds
⅓ cup milk
1 egg
2 tablespoons salad oil

Into mixing bowl sift flour, sugar, baking powder, and salt; set aside. Place apricots in blender container. In saucepan heat nectar to boiling; pour over apricots. Cool to lukewarm. Add almonds, milk, egg, and oil to apricots in blender container. Blend till apricots and nuts are coarsely chopped. Pour apricot mixture over dry ingredients. Stir just to moisten. Turn batter into greased and floured 9x5x3-inch loaf pan. Bake at 350° for 1 hour. Cool 10 minutes before removing from pan. Makes 1.

PEANUT BUTTER MUFFINS

Make your own fresh peanut butter in the blender as the first step to these delectable muffins—

2 cups sifted all-purpose flour
3 teaspoons baking powder
1 cup salted peanuts* *or* ½ cup peanut
    butter
1 cup milk
2 eggs
½ cup sugar
1 teaspoon salt

In mixing bowl sift together flour and baking powder; set aside. Place peanuts in blender container; adjust lid. Blend at low speed until finely chopped. Change to high speed and blend till smooth. (When necessary, stop blender and use rubber spatula to scrape down sides.) Add milk, eggs, sugar, and salt to mixture in blender container; blend to combine.

Pour peanut butter mixture over dry ingredients; mix just to moisten the dry ingredients. Fill greased muffin pans ⅔ full. Bake in a 400° oven for 15 to 20 minutes. Makes 12.

*If dry roasted peanuts are used, 1 tablespoon salad oil should be added to nuts.

BANANA-OATMEAL MUFFINS

1 cup sifted all-purpose flour
3 tablespoons sugar
3 teaspoons baking powder
½ teaspoon salt
1 cup quick-cooking rolled oats
¼ cup milk
1 egg
2 tablespoons salad oil
1 large ripe banana

Into large mixing bowl sift together flour, sugar, baking powder, and salt. Stir in rolled oats. Put milk, egg, and salad oil in blender container. Holding peeled banana over blender, cut fruit into container. Blend till mixture is smooth. Pour banana mixture over dry ingredients; stir just enough to moisten dry ingredients. Fill greased muffin pans ⅔ full. Bake at 425° for 20 to 25 minutes. Makes 8 to 10.

SPICY APPLE MUFFINS

      2 cups sifted all-purpose flour
      3 teaspoons baking powder
      1 teaspoon salt
      ½ teaspoon ground cinnamon
      ¼ teaspoon ground nutmeg
      ⅔ cup milk
      2 eggs
      ¼ cup salad oil
      ⅔ cup brown sugar
      1 medium apple, peeled, cut in
        eighths, and cored
      ¼ cup walnuts
      1 cup whole wheat flakes *or* bran
        flakes

In large mixing bowl sift together flour, baking powder, salt, cinnamon, and nutmeg; set aside. Put milk, eggs, oil, and brown sugar in blender container; blend till well mixed. Add apple pieces and nuts; blend till coarsely chopped. Pour apple mixture over dry ingredients; stir just to moisten. Fold in cereal flakes. Fill greased muffin pans ⅔ full. Bake at 400° for 15 to 20 minutes. Makes 12 muffins.

CARROT MUFFINS

The delicate fresh carrot flavor and golden hue give these muffins special appeal—

      1¾ cups sifted all-purpose flour
      2½ teaspoons baking powder
      1 teaspoon salt
      ⅔ cup milk
      ⅓ cup salad oil
      1 egg
      ¼ cup sugar
      2 medium carrots, sliced

Sift flour, baking powder, and salt together in mixing bowl; set aside.

   Place milk, oil, egg, sugar, and carrots in blender container; blend till carrots are very finely chopped. Pour carrot mixture over dry ingredients. Mix just enough to moisten dry ingredients. Spoon mixture into greased muffin pans, filling ⅔ full. Bake in a 425° oven for about 25 minutes. Makes 8 to 10 muffins.

ORANGE-CURRANT MUFFINS

      1¾ cups sifted all-purpose flour
      ¼ cup sugar
      2½ teaspoons baking powder
      ¾ teaspoon salt
      ¾ cup currants
      ½ cup milk
      1 egg
      ⅓ cup salad oil
      ¼ cup orange juice
      1 1-inch square piece orange peel

In a mixing bowl sift together the flour, sugar, baking powder, and salt. Stir the currants into the flour mixture; set aside.

   Place the milk, egg, salad oil, orange juice, and square of orange peel in the blender container; adjust lid. Blend till orange peel is finely chopped and ingredients are combined. Pour the orange mixture over the dry ingredients; stir just until moistened.

   Fill paper-lined muffin cups or greased muffin pans ⅔ full. Bake at 400° for 20 to 25 minutes. Serve warm. Makes 12 muffins.

COFFEE-DATE MUFFINS

Chop dates and combine liquids in one action—

      1¾ cups sifted all-purpose flour
      2½ teaspoons baking powder
      1 cup water
      1 egg
      ⅓ cup salad oil
      ¼ cup sugar
      1½ teaspoons instant coffee powder
      ¾ teaspoon salt
      1 8-ounce package pitted dates

Sift the flour and the baking powder together into a mixing bowl; set aside.

   Place water, egg, salad oil, sugar, instant coffee powder, salt, and dates in blender container. Blend till ingredients are mixed and the dates are coarsely chopped. Pour date mixture over dry ingredients. Stir just till dry ingredients are moistened. Fill paper bake cups or greased muffin pans about ⅔ full. Bake in a 400° oven about 25 minutes. Makes 12.

POPOVERS

    1 cup milk
    3 eggs
    1 tablespoon salad oil
  ½ teaspoon salt
    1 cup sifted all-purpose flour

Place the milk, eggs, oil, and salt in blender container. Blend at high speed until well mixed. Add the flour to mixture in the blender container; blend just until batter is smooth.

  Pour batter into well-greased muffin or custard cups, filling ½ full. Bake at 475° for 15 minutes; reduce to 350° and bake 25 to 30 minutes longer. A few minutes before removing from oven, prick popovers with a fork to let steam escape. Serve hot. Makes 6 to 8.

TOMATO-CHEESE MUFFINS

So-good-together flavors blended in a tender hot bread for lunch or dinner—

1¾ cups sifted all-purpose flour
  2 teaspoons baking powder
 ½ teaspoon baking soda
 ¾ cup tomato juice
  1 egg
 ⅛ cup salad oil
  2 tablespoons sugar
 ½ teaspoon salt
  4 ounces process American cheese, cut
     in cubes (½ cup)

Sift first 3 ingredients into a mixing bowl; set aside. Put tomato juice, egg, salad oil, sugar, salt, and cheese in blender container. Blend till cheese is finely chopped. Pour tomato mixture over dry ingredients; stir just till moistened. Fill paper-lined muffin pans ⅔ full. Bake at 400° for 25 minutes. Makes 12 muffins.

Hot from the oven

Pass butter with these crusty Popovers or break them open and spoon creamed meat or seafood mixtures into the hollow centers.

COTTAGE CHEESE PANCAKES

Try topping these delicate hot cakes with sliced oranges and shredded coconut—

1½ cups milk
1 egg
¾ cup cream-style cottage cheese
2 tablespoons butter or
    margarine, softened
1 1-inch square piece orange peel
1½ cups packaged pancake mix
2 large oranges, peeled and cut in
    thin cartwheel slices
    Sugar
    Butter or margarine
    Shredded coconut

Place milk, egg, cottage cheese, butter or margarine, and orange peel in blender container. Blend till mixture is smooth and orange peel is finely chopped. Add pancake mix to blender container. Blend just till pancake mix is moistened. (Mixture will not be smooth.) Bake on lightly greased griddle, using ¼ cup batter for each pancake. Makes 12 pancakes.

Heat orange slices in saucepan; sweeten with sugar, if desired. At serving time, butter the pancakes generously. Arrange on plates in stacks of three each. Spoon orange slices over. Sprinkle coconut on top. Serves 4.

BREAD CRUMB PANCAKES

A tasty use for leftover dry bread—

2 slices dry bread
1½ cups buttermilk
2 eggs
2 tablespoons salad oil
1½ cups sifted all-purpose flour
1 teaspoon baking soda
½ teaspoon salt

Break dry bread slices into blender container; blend till in coarse dry crumbs. Add remaining ingredients to bread in blender container; blend just to combine. Drop batter by tablespoons on hot, lightly greased griddle. (Small cakes are easier to manage.) Makes 2 dozen.

FEATHER-LIGHT PANCAKES

Give these pancakes a delightful smoky flavor by substituting bacon drippings for salad oil—

1 cup milk
1 egg
2 tablespoons salad oil
1 cup sifted all-purpose flour
2 tablespoons baking powder
2 tablespoons sugar
½ teaspoon salt

Put all ingredients in blender container; blend till smooth. Bake on hot griddle. Makes 12 silver-dollar size or eight 4-inch pancakes.

FRENCH PANCAKES (CREPES)

¾ cup milk
1 egg
1 egg yolk
1 tablespoon butter or margarine,
    melted
⅛ cup sifted all-purpose flour
1 tablespoon sugar
    Dash salt
    Jelly *or* sweetened fresh fruit
    Sifted confectioners' sugar

Put first 7 ingredients in blender container. Blend till batter is smooth.

Lightly grease a 6-inch skillet; heat till drop of water dances on surface. Lift skillet off heat and pour 2 tablespoons batter into it. Tilt skillet from side to side till batter covers bottom evenly. Return skillet to heat and cook pancake till underside is lightly browned, about 1½ minutes. To remove, invert skillet over paper toweling. Keep warm till served. Repeat with remaining pancake batter.

Spread unbrowned side of pancakes with the jelly or spoon sweetened fruit down the center. Roll up and place pancakes, folded side down, on heated platter. Sprinkle tops lightly with confectioners' sugar. Makes 10. *Special serving hint:* Turn French Pancakes into an elegant entree. Instead of jelly or fruit, fill with diced chicken or shrimp and top with a rich cream sauce. Serve from a chafing dish.

Blender tip: Combine liquid and chop fruit or nuts in one step when making nutbreads and muffins in the blender. Stir blended ingredients into sifted ingredients.

GINGERBREAD WAFFLES

½ cup water
½ cup salad oil
2 eggs
½ cup light molasses
1½ cups sifted all-purpose flour
1½ teaspoons baking powder
½ teaspoon baking soda
½ teaspoon salt
½ teaspoon ground cinnamon
½ teaspoon ground ginger
¼ teaspoon ground nutmeg
½ cup nuts

Place water, salad oil, eggs, and molasses in blender container; blend until mixed. Add flour, baking powder, baking soda, salt, cinnamon, ginger, nutmeg, and nuts. Blend just till nuts are coarsely chopped. Bake in waffle baker until crisp. Makes 3 large waffles.

BELGIAN WAFFLES

Brunch or dessert waffles decked with luscious strawberries and capped with ice cream—

2 cups fresh strawberries
2 tablespoons sugar
½ cup milk
1 egg
3 tablespoons salad oil
1 cup dairy sour cream
1 cup sifted all-purpose flour
2 teaspoons sugar
1 teaspoon baking powder
¼ teaspoon baking soda
¼ teaspoon salt
1 pint vanilla ice cream, softened

Put *1 cup* of the strawberries and *1 tablespoon* of the sugar in blender container. Blend just till berries are coarsely crushed. Empty container. Repeat with the remaining berries and the sugar. Set strawberry sauce aside.

Place milk, egg, salad oil, and sour cream in blender container; blend to mix. Add the flour, sugar, baking powder, baking soda, and salt; blend at low speed just till ingredients are combined. Bake in preheated waffle baker till crisp. Spoon strawberry sauce over the waffles. Top the waffles with spoonfuls of softened ice cream. Makes two 10-inch waffles.

PEANUT BUTTER WAFFLES

Stack sandwich-fashion with jelly in between—

1 cup milk
1 egg
2 tablespoons salad oil
⅛ cup chunk-style peanut butter
2 tablespoons sugar
1 cup packaged pancake mix
Butter
Jelly

Place first 6 ingredients in blender container; blend just to combine ingredients and moisten pancake mix. (Mixture will not be smooth.) Bake in preheated waffle baker. Serve with butter and jelly. Makes 32 small waffles.

STEP-SHORTENED DESSERTS

Analyze dessert recipes and you will be surprised at the amount of chopping and blending that go into even the easiest nut- or crumb-topped creation. As masterpieces become more complicated, the blender simplifies the jobs to be done.

Save yourself time by blender-chopping or purreeing the fruits needed, such as bananas, strawberries, apricots, peaches, dates, and cranberries. Dissolve both flavored and unflavored gelatins or combine eggs, milk, and spices or flavorings as the first step in preparing a tempting array of pies, cookies, puddings, and frozen concoctions.

MOCHA ROLL

    4 eggs
    ½ teaspoon salt
    ¾ cup sugar
    1 teaspoon vanilla
    ¾ cup packaged pancake mix
       Confectioners' sugar
 1½ cups milk
    1 4½-ounce package *instant* chocolate
       pudding mix
    1 tablespoon instant coffee powder
       Sifted confectioners' sugar
       Shaved chocolate

Place eggs and salt in blender container; blend till frothy. Add sugar and vanilla; blend till smooth and thick. Add pancake mix; blend to combine. Spread in greased and floured 15½x 10½x1-inch pan. Bake at 400° for 8 to 10 minutes. Loosen sides; turn out onto towel dusted with confectioners' sugar. Starting at narrow end, roll cake and towel; cool.

Place milk, *instant* chocolate pudding mix, and coffee powder in blender container; blend till ingredients are thoroughly combined.

Unroll cooled cake; spread with mocha filling. Reroll and chill. At serving time sprinkle with sifted confectioners' sugar and top with shaved chocolate. Makes 10 servings.

MENU

Pot Roast Stroganoff*
Hot Noodles
Lettuce   Confetti Dressing
Mocha Roll*
Beverage

*See index listing for page number.

FLAN

    ⅓ cup sugar
    2 14½-ounce cans evaporated milk
    4 eggs
    2 teaspoons vanilla
    ½ cup sugar

In 8-inch skillet caramelize the ⅓ cup sugar by heating and stirring it over medium heat until it is melted and golden brown in color. Quickly pour into an 8-inch round baking dish, tilting the dish so that the caramelized mixture spreads over the entire bottom.

Place the milk, eggs, vanilla, and the ½ cup sugar in blender container. Blend to combine. Pour the custard mixture into the caramel-coated baking dish. Set baking dish in a larger pan. Add boiling water to the outer pan to a depth of 1 inch. Bake at 325° till a knife inserted halfway between the center and the edge of the flan comes out clean, about 45 minutes. (Center will be soft.) Chill. Carefully loosen sides and invert on platter. Serves 8.

Pinwheel slices

Both cake and filling for a Mocha Roll are →
blender-made from mixes. The cake uses pancake mix and the filling instant pudding.

MOLDED APRICOT CREAM

Tempting dessert featured on the front cover—

    1 envelope unflavored gelatin
    ¼ cup cold water
    1 3-ounce package orange-flavored
        gelatin
    ¾ cup boiling water
    1 17-ounce can apricot halves,
        undrained
    1 pint vanilla ice cream
        Vanilla Dessert Sauce (*see page 63*)
        Seedless green grapes

Put unflavored gelatin and cold water in blender container; let stand to soften gelatin. Add orange-flavored gelatin and boiling water; blend at low speed until gelatins are dissolved. Add apricots. Blend till pureed.

Add ice cream, a spoonful at a time, blending smooth after each addition. Pour into 4½-cup mold. Refrigerate until firm, 6 to 8 hours or overnight. Unmold on platter to serve. Spoon Vanilla Dessert Sauce over top. Garnish with grapes, if desired. Serves 4 to 6.

BLENDER POTS DE CRÈME

    ¼ cup cold water
    1½ envelopes unflavored gelatin
    2 teaspoons instant coffee powder
    ½ cup hot milk
    1 6-ounce package semisweet
        chocolate pieces
    1 tablespoon sugar
        Dash salt
    ½ teaspoon vanilla
    2 egg yolks
    1¼ cups *drained* finely crushed ice
    1 cup whipping cream

Put first 3 ingredients in blender container; let stand to soften gelatin. Add milk to blender; blend till gelatin is dissolved. Add chocolate, sugar, salt, and vanilla to blender; blend smooth. Add egg yolks and ice; blend till smooth. With blender slowly running, add cream. Blend till it *begins* to thicken. Pour into sherbets. Chill 10 minutes. Serves 5 to 6.

THREE-FRUIT SHERBET

    ½ cup whipping cream
    1 ripe banana, cut in pieces
    ½ 6-ounce can frozen orange juice
        concentrate, slightly thawed
    1 13½-ounce can frozen pineapple
        chunks, broken into pieces

Put all ingredients into blender container; blend just till combined. Spoon into freezer tray; freeze till firm. Serves 6.

GINGER-PEACHY FREEZE

    5 gingersnaps
    1 cup whipping cream
    2 medium fresh peaches, peeled and
        quartered
    ½ cup sugar
    ½ teaspoon vanilla

Break gingersnaps into blender. Add remaining ingredients; blend till smooth and mixture is thickened. Spoon into freezer tray; freeze till firm. Remove to chilled bowl; beat till fluffy. Return to tray; freeze firm. Serves 6.

PEPPERMINT ICE CREAM

    1 8½-ounce package hard peppermint
        candy
    1½ teaspoons unflavored gelatin
    2 cups milk
    ½ teaspoon salt
    2 cups whipping cream
        Few drops red food coloring

Put 8 candies in blender; blend to crush. Empty. Repeat. In saucepan soften gelatin in milk; heat and stir to dissolve gelatin. Reserve ¼ cup crushed candy. Add remainder with salt to hot mixture; stir till dissolved. Pour into two freezer trays. Freeze firm.

In mixer bowl break frozen mixture into chunks. Beat till smooth. Whip cream till soft peaks form; fold into mixture with reserved ¼ cup candy. Tint with food coloring, if desired. Return to trays; freeze till firm. Serves 6 to 8.

Blender tip: Dissolve flavored gelatin in hot water in blender at low speed. Quick-set the gelatin by adding ice cubes, one at a time, to equal the remaining water needed. Allow 6 ice cubes per cup of water.

BERRY-GELATIN DESSERT

    1 3-ounce package strawberry-flavored
         gelatin
    ½ cup boiling water
    6 ice cubes
    1 10-ounce package frozen strawberries,
         broken into chunks
    1 cup frozen dessert topping, thawed

Place gelatin and boiling water in blender container. Blend at low speed till gelatin is dissolved. Add *one* of the ice cubes to blender; blend till chopped and melted. Repeat with remaining ice cubes till mixture is cool.

Add strawberries to mixture in blender container; blend until frozen chunks are dissolved. Pour mixture into mixing bowl. Let stand 5 minutes. Fold in dessert topping. Spoon into sherbets. Makes 6 servings.

FROZEN PINEAPPLE DESSERT

    36 vanilla wafers
     4 tablespoons butter, melted
     3 egg yolks
     1 15-ounce can sweetened condensed
          milk
     1 6-ounce can frozen pineapple juice,
          thawed
     2 tablespoons lemon juice
     3 egg whites
              • • •
     1 tablespoon cornstarch
     2 tablespoons water
     1 10-ounce package frozen raspberries,
          thawed
     3 tablespoons sugar

Break 6 or 7 vanilla wafers into blender container; blend to fine crumbs. Transfer to mixing bowl. Repeat with remaining wafers. Toss crumbs with butter. Reserve ⅓ cup crumbs; pat remainder into 8x8x2-inch dish. Chill.

Put egg yolks, milk, pineapple juice, and lemon juice in blender container; blend till mixture is smooth. Beat egg whites till stiff peaks form. Fold condensed milk mixture into egg whites. Pour over crumbs in pan. Top with reserved crumbs. Freeze 8 hours.

In saucepan combine cornstarch and water. Add berries and syrup. Cook and stir till thickened and bubbly. Remove from heat. Strain, discarding seeds. Stir in sugar; cool. Cut dessert in squares just before serving. Top with sauce. Makes 9 servings.

BOYSENBERRY SORBET

    2 10-ounce packages frozen
         boysenberries, partially thawed
    ⅓ cup cold water
    ¼ cup orange-flavored liqueur
    2 teaspoons lemon juice

Cube or break apart boysenberries into blender container. Add remaining ingredients; blend at high speed till smooth yet slushy. Pour into freezer tray. Freeze till firm. Remove from freezer 10 minutes before serving; spoon into sherbet dishes. Serves 6 to 8.

CRANBERRY-CHEESE PIE

1 15-ounce can sweetened *condensed* milk
⅓ cup lemon juice
½ teaspoon vanilla
1 8-ounce package cream cheese, cut in cubes and softened
1 16-ounce can whole cranberry sauce
1 9-inch Vanilla Wafer Crust, chilled
Whipped cream

Put milk, lemon juice, vanilla, and cheese in the blender container; blend till mixture is smooth. Set aside a few whole cranberries from sauce. Fold remaining sauce into cheese mixture. Spoon into crust. Freeze till firm. Remove from freezer 10 minutes before serving. Top with whipped cream and garnish with the reserved cranberries.

MINCE CREAM PIE

In-a-hurry version of a holiday specialty—

Piecrust mix for one 8-inch pie shell
1½ cups prepared mincemeat
1 3x1½-inch strip orange peel
1 3¾- or 3⅝-ounce package *instant* vanilla pudding mix
1½ cups milk
Ground nutmeg

Prepare pie shell according to package directions. Bake; cool. Spoon mincemeat into piecrust. Put orange peel in blender container; blend till finely chopped. Add pudding mix and milk to blender container; blend till combined. Pour pudding mixture over mincemeat. Sprinkle top lightly with nutmeg. Chill.

Combine cream cheese and cranberry sauce in blender to make this Cranberry-Cheese Pie. The pie filling is chilled in a blender-made Vanilla Wafer Crust.

ORANGE-PECAN PIE

Piecrust mix for one 9-inch pie
  shell
1 medium orange
3 eggs
1 cup dark corn syrup
⅔ cup sugar
¼ cup butter or margarine,
  melted
Dash salt
1 cup whole pecans

Prepare pie shell according to package directions. Do not bake. Peel orange, reserving 1-inch square. Quarter orange; remove seeds.

Put orange pieces, orange peel, eggs, corn syrup, sugar, butter, and salt in blender container. Blend till mixture is smooth and light colored and the orange peel is finely chopped.

Sprinkle pecans evenly in bottom of pie shell; pour blender mixture over pecans. Bake at 350° till knife inserted off-center comes out clean, about 60 minutes. Cool.

PUMPKIN PARFAIT PIE

4 teaspoons unflavored gelatin
¼ cup cold water
½ cup brown sugar
1 teaspoon instant coffee powder
½ teaspoon ground cinnamon
½ teaspoon ground ginger
¼ teaspoon ground nutmeg
¾ cup boiling water
1 pint vanilla ice cream
1 cup canned pumpkin
1 9-inch Graham Cracker Crust

Place gelatin and cold water in blender container. Allow to stand a few minutes to soften gelatin. Add brown sugar, coffee powder, cinnamon, ginger, nutmeg, and boiling water to blender container. Blend at low speed till gelatin, coffee powder, and brown sugar are dissolved. Add ice cream, a spoonful at a time, blending till smooth after each addition. Add pumpkin; blend till smooth and well distributed. Chill till it mounds when spooned, about 5 minutes. Spoon into crust. Chill.

VANILLA WAFER CRUST

36 vanilla wafers
6 tablespoons butter or margarine,
  melted

Break 6 or 7 wafers into blender container; blend to fine crumbs. Set aside. Repeat to make 1½ cups crumbs. Mix butter with crumbs. Press into a 9-inch pie plate. Chill.

CHOCOLATE WAFER CRUST

24 chocolate wafers
6 tablespoons butter or margarine,
  melted

Break 6 wafers into blender container; blend to make fine crumbs. Set aside. Repeat to make 1½ cups crumbs. Mix butter with crumbs. Press into 9-inch pie plate. Chill.

GRAHAM CRACKER CRUST

16 graham crackers
¼ cup sugar
6 tablespoons butter or margarine,
  melted

Break 6 or 7 crackers into blender container; blend to make fine crumbs. Set aside in bowl. Repeat to make 1¼ cups crumbs. Combine sugar and melted butter or margarine with crumbs. Press firmly into 9-inch pie plate.

For baked crust: Bake at 375° till edges of crust are browned, about 6 to 8 minutes.

For unbaked crust: Chill 45 minutes.

GINGERSNAP CRUST

20 gingersnaps
¼ cup butter or margarine, softened

Break 6 to 7 gingersnaps into blender container; blend to make fine crumbs. Set aside. Repeat to make 1½ cups crumbs. Mix butter with crumbs. Press firmly into buttered 9-inch pie plate. Bake at 375° about 8 minutes. Cool.

LEMON BARS DELUXE

    2 cups sifted all-purpose flour
    ½ cup sifted confectioners' sugar
    1 cup butter or margarine
    4 eggs
    2 cups granulated sugar
    ⅓ cup lemon juice
    ¼ cup all-purpose flour
    ½ teaspoon baking powder
      Sifted confectioners' sugar

Sift together the first 2 ingredients. Cut in butter till mixture clings together. Press in 13x9x 2-inch baking pan. Bake at 350° till lightly browned, about 20 to 25 minutes.

Put eggs, 2 cups sugar, and lemon juice in blender; blend till thick and smooth. Sift ¼ cup flour and baking powder. Add to blender; blend to combine. Pour over crust. Bake at 350° for 25 minutes. Sprinkle with confectioners' sugar. Cool. Cut in bars. Makes 30.

REFRIGERATOR FRUITCAKE

    1 pound graham crackers
    ½ cup pecans
    3 tablespoons water
    ½ cup orange marmalade
    ¼ cup light corn syrup
    ½ cup confectioners' sugar
    ½ cup butter or margarine, softened
    1 teaspoon ground cinnamon
    ¾ teaspoon ground cloves
    ½ teaspoon salt
   16 ounces mixed candied fruits and
        peels (2 cups)
   1½ cups raisins
    1 cup pitted dates

Break 6 or 7 crackers into blender; blend till finely crushed. Set aside. Repeat. Put nuts in blender; blend till coarsely chopped. Toss with crumbs. Put next 8 ingredients in blender; blend till combined. Pour over crumbs; mix.

Combine mixed candied fruits and peels, raisins, and dates; add to cracker mixture. Pack mixture into one 9x5x3-inch loaf pan *or* two 7½x3¾x2¼-inch loaf pans lined with waxed paper. Refrigerate 24 hours.

HOLIDAY CARROT PUDDING

   1¼ cups sifted all-purpose flour
    1 teaspoon baking powder
    ½ teaspoon baking soda
    ½ teaspoon ground cinnamon
    ½ teaspoon ground nutmeg
    2 eggs
    ½ cup shortening
    ¾ cup brown sugar
    1 medium apple, peeled, cut in
        eighths, and cored
    2 medium carrots, sliced
    1 potato, peeled and cut in pieces
    ¾ cup raisins
      Brandy Hard Sauce

Sift together first 5 ingredients in mixing bowl. Place eggs, shortening, and sugar in blender container; blend till smooth. Add apple; blend till finely chopped. Add carrot slices; blend till coarsely chopped. Add potato pieces; blend till finely chopped. Add blender mixture and raisins to dry ingredients; mix well. Spoon into greased and floured 4-cup mold. Cover tightly. Place on rack in deep kettle; add water 1-inch deep. Cover kettle; steam for 2½ hours. Cool 10 to 15 minutes. Unmold. Serve with Brandy Hard Sauce.

BOURBON BALLS

   60 vanilla wafers
    ½ cup walnuts
    1 cup sifted confectioners' sugar
    2 tablespoons unsweetened cocoa
        powder
    ¼ cup bourbon
    ¼ cup light corn syrup
      Granulated sugar

Break 6 vanilla wafers into blender; blend to make fine crumbs. Transfer to bowl. Repeat. Put nuts in blender; blend till chopped. Add to crumbs. Combine confectioners' sugar and cocoa with crumbs. Stir in bourbon and corn syrup. If necessary, add about 1¼ teaspoons of water so that mixture will shape. Form into ¾-inch balls. Roll in granulated sugar. Store in tightly covered container. Makes 4 dozen.

BRANDY HARD SAUCE

  2 tablespoons brandy *or* rum
  ⅛ cup very soft butter
  1 cup sifted confectioners' sugar
     Ground nutmeg

Place brandy and soft butter in blender container; blend to combine. Add the sifted confectioners' sugar to blender container. Blend till smooth. Spoon mixture into mold or small bowl. Chill. At serving time unmold and sprinkle surface lightly with ground nutmeg.
Special cooking hint: If you prefer to use light cream instead of the brandy or rum, add vanilla or rum flavoring to taste.

ALMOND BALLS

  ½ cup blanched almonds
  ¾ cup butter or margarine
  ⅓ cup sifted confectioners' sugar
  1 teaspoon vanilla
  2 cups sifted all-purpose flour
  ¼ teaspoon salt
     Sifted confectioners' sugar

Put almonds in blender container; blend till finely chopped. Cream butter, sugar, and vanilla. Combine flour, salt, and nuts; add to creamed mixture. Mix well. Shape in 1-inch balls. Bake on greased cookie sheet at 325° for 20 minutes. Cool. Roll in sugar. Makes 48.

Welcome your holiday guests with this quartet of festive goodies—Lemon Bars Deluxe, Almond Balls, Refrigerator Fruitcake, and Bourbon Balls.

APRICOT SLICES

    16 graham crackers
    ½ cup walnuts
     1 cup dried apricots
     2 tablespoons butter or margarine
     2 eggs
    ½ cup granulated sugar
    ½ cup brown sugar
     1 teaspoon vanilla
     1 cup coconut

Break 5 or 6 crackers into blender container; blend to fine crumbs. Set aside. Repeat. Put nuts in blender; blend till coarsely chopped. Add to crumbs. Put apricots in blender; blend till finely chopped. Melt butter in large skillet. Add apricots and stir. Put eggs and sugars in blender; blend smooth. Add to apricots. Cook over low heat; stir till sugars melt and mixture is thick and bubbly, 10 to 15 minutes. Remove from heat; stir in vanilla, crumbs, nuts, and coconut. Shape two 7-inch rolls. Wrap; chill and slice. Makes 3½ dozen.

SPICY RAISIN BARS

     1 cup raisins
     1 cup hot water
    1¾ cups sifted all-purpose flour
     1 teaspoon baking soda
    ¼ teaspoon salt
     1 teaspoon ground cinnamon
    ½ teaspoon ground nutmeg
    ½ teaspoon ground allspice
    ¼ teaspoon ground cloves
    ½ cup salad oil
     1 cup sugar
     1 egg
    ½ cup walnuts
       Sifted confectioners' sugar

Put raisins in blender. Add water; cool. Sift together flour, soda, and spices. Set aside.

Add next 4 ingredients to raisins in blender container; blend just till nuts are coarsely chopped. Pour over dry ingredients; mix well. Pour into greased 15½x10½x1-inch baking pan. Bake at 375° about 12 minutes. Cool; cut in bars. Dust with sugar. Makes 4 dozen.

ANISE SUGAR COOKIES

Spinning aniseed and sugar in the blender crushes the seed and distributes the delicate licorice flavor in one easy operation—

     6 vanilla wafers
     1 tablespoon sugar
    3½ cups sifted all-purpose flour
     1 teaspoon baking soda
    ½ teaspoon baking powder
     2 teaspoons whole aniseed
     1 cup sugar
    ½ cup shortening
     2 eggs
     1 cup dairy sour cream
     2 tablespoons butter or margarine,
       melted

Break the vanilla wafers into blender container. Adjust lid; blend till wafers are finely crushed. Transfer to small mixing bowl. Stir in the 1 tablespoon sugar and set aside.

In large mixing bowl sift together flour, baking soda, and baking powder.

Place aniseed and the 1 cup sugar in blender container; blend at high speed till aniseed is crushed. Add the shortening and eggs to blender container; blend till thick and smooth. Add sour cream; blend just till combined. Stir sour cream mixture into dry ingredients. Mix well and chill dough thoroughly.

Using one-half the dough at a time, roll out on floured pastry cloth or board to a 12x16-inch rectangle, ⅛ inch thick. Brush rolled out dough with half the melted butter. Sprinkle with ½ the crumb mixture. Cut into 2x3-inch rectangles. Place on ungreased baking sheet. Bake at 375° till lightly browned, about 8 to 10 minutes. Repeat with remaining dough, butter, and crumbs. Cool. Makes 60.

WHITE SUGAR COOKIES

Follow recipe for Anise Sugar Cookies, omitting the aniseed and adding 1 teaspoon of vanilla to the sour cream. Roll dough to ⅛-inch thickness for thin, crisp cookies. Roll to ¼-inch thickness for bigger, softer cookies. Cut in rectangles or use shaped cookie cutters.

TRIFLE

Make this famous British specialty in your prettiest glass bowl or prepare in individual dessert dishes as pictured on page 33—

    1 loaf pound cake
    ½ cup raspberry preserves
    1 17-ounce can apricot halves,
         drained
    ½ cup sherry
       Vanilla Dessert Sauce
    ¼ cup walnuts
    ½ cup whipping cream

Slice pound cake horizontally into 4 layers; spread two layers with preserves. Top each with one of remaining layers. Cut into 16 finger sandwiches. Put apricots in blender container; blend till coarsely chopped.

Assemble dessert using either of the methods below. Chill 8 hours or overnight. Before serving put walnuts in blender container; blend till coarsely chopped. Whip cream. Top Trifle with cream and nuts. Serves 8 to 10.

To assemble in serving bowl: Place *half* the sandwiches spoke-fashion in bottom of 2-quart bowl. Sprinkle with *half* of the sherry. Place remaining sandwiches on top; sprinkle with remaining sherry. Spoon apricots over cake. Pour Vanilla Dessert Sauce over dessert.

To assemble as individual desserts: Trim sandwiches to fit dishes. Sprinkle each dessert with about 1 tablespoon sherry. Spoon apricots over cake. Spoon Vanilla Dessert Sauce over.

VANILLA DESSERT SAUCE

A versatile sauce with a rich and custardlike consistency so right as a dessert topping—

    2¾ cups milk
     1 3¾- or 3⅝-ounce package *instant*
          vanilla pudding mix
     ½ teaspoon vanilla

Put all ingredients in blender container; blend at high speed about 30 seconds. Pour into pitcher. Chill, if desired. Pour over sweetened fruit or other dessert. Makes 2¾ cups sauce.

FRESH APPLESAUCE

    4 medium apples
    ¼ cup water
    2 tablespoons lemon juice
    ¼ cup sugar

Peel, core, and cube apples. Put water, lemon juice, apples, and sugar in blender container; blend till smooth. Serve immediately. (Or transfer to saucepan; bring to boiling to keep apples from darkening.) Makes 2 cups.

Special cooking tip: To make pink applesauce tint with a few drops of red food coloring *or* add 1 tablespoon red cinnamon candies and heat long enough to dissolve candies.

CHOCO-BLENDER FROSTING

    1 cup sugar
    3 1-ounce squares unsweetened
         chocolate, cut in pieces
    1 6-ounce can evaporated milk
       Dash salt

Put sugar in blender container; blend at high speed about 1 minute. Add chocolate pieces, evaporated milk, and salt. Blend at high speed till thick enough for spreading consistency, about 3 minutes. (When necessary, stop blender and use rubber spatula to scrape down sides.) Makes frosting for tops of two 8-inch layers. For firmer frosting, chill frosted cake.

CREAM CHEESE FROSTING

    1 teaspoon milk
    1 3-ounce package cream cheese, cut
         in cubes and softened
    1 tablespoon butter, softened
    1 teaspoon vanilla
    2 cups sifted confectioners' sugar

Put first 4 ingredients in blender container; blend till smooth. Add *1 cup* of confectioners' sugar to blender; blend till smooth. Add ¼ cup sugar; blend till smooth. Repeat with remaining sugar till mixture is of spreading consistency. Frosts one 8- or 9-inch square cake.

Giving a party is a particular pleasure for the host and hostess who use a blender. Even before the guests arrive, this portable helper goes right to work.

You can use the blender to make smooth dips and elegant pâtés to pass with crisp crackers and vegetable dippers. Why not concoct a peppy sauce for cooked shrimp, or blend together Cheddar, blue, and cottage cheese and shape them into a fancy cheese ball? And make the filling for deviled eggs or build a many-layered sandwich loaf.

At party time move the blender where your guests are congregated and show off its drink-making abilities by fixing popular cocktails to order, or by filling the punch bowl with a sparkling fruit drink or cheery party beverage.

Serve Snow-Capped Pâté, Pineapple-Melon Punch, Shrimp Dip, Applejack Flip, Bacardi Cocktail, Frozen Daiquiri, Ramoz Fizz, and Tom Collins.

Party foods and drinks

REFRESHING DRINKS AND PUNCHES

Master the art of mixing festive drinks in your blender, and assure yourself of success as a party-giver. Include both alcoholic and nonalcoholic specialties in your repertoire. Chill blender container and ingredients so each drink will be icy cold.

CRANBERRY PUNCH

Honey and rum flavoring are the flavor secrets—

    4 quarts cranberry-apple drink,
        chilled
    2 to 3 tablespoons rum flavoring
    ½ cup honey
      Ice ring

Put *1 quart* of the chilled cranberry-apple drink, rum flavoring, and honey in blender container; blend till combined. Add to remaining cranberry-apple drink in large punch bowl; stir till blended. Carefully slip ice ring into the punch in bowl. Makes 4 quarts.

FRUITED TEA PUNCH

Citrus fruit drink with a delicate tea flavor—

    3 tablespoons instant tea powder
    ½ cup sugar
    ⅓ cup lime juice
    3 tablespoons lemon juice
    4 cups cold water
      Ice
      Lime slices
      Maraschino cherries

Put first 4 ingredients and *2 cups* of the water in blender; blend till combined. Pour mixture into a pitcher. Add remaining water; stir. Serve over ice in tall glasses. Garnish with lime slices and cherries. Makes 1¼ quarts.

MENU

Shrimp Cocktail Dip*
Snow-Capped Pâté*
Pineapple-Melon Punch*
Assorted Cocktails
Nuts   Mints

*See index listing for page number.

RASPBERRY CRUSH

    4 cups cold water
    1 envelope unsweetened raspberry-
        flavored soft drink powder
    ½ cup sugar
    1 6-ounce can frozen lemonade
        concentrate
    1 10-ounce package frozen raspberries,
        thawed
    1 28-ounce bottle lemon-lime
        carbonated beverage
      Ice cubes

Put *2 cups* of the cold water, raspberry-flavored soft drink powder, sugar, and frozen lemonade concentrate in blender container; blend till powder and sugar are dissolved.

Combine mixture with remaining 2 cups water and thawed raspberries. Stir. Chill. Just before serving, gently stir in carbonated beverage. Serve over ice. Makes 2¼ quarts.

Pick your favorite

Enjoy cool Cranberry Punch, Lime-Apple → Cooler, Fruited Tea Punch, Spiced Fruit Sparkle, or Raspberry Crush on a hot day.

LIME-APPLE COOLER

3 cups apple juice, chilled
1 cup water
1 6-ounce can frozen limeade
    concentrate
Few drops green food coloring
4 to 5 ice cubes

Put first 4 ingredients in blender container; blend till mixture is frothy. Add ice cubes (*see tip, page 69*). Makes 1 quart.

PINEAPPLE-MELON PUNCH

1 medium cantaloupe, halved, seeded,
    peeled, and cut up
1 tablespoon lemon juice
8 maraschino cherries, drained
1 46-ounce can pineapple juice,
    chilled
2 7-ounce bottles ginger ale,
    chilled
  Ice

Put first 3 ingredients in blender container; add pineapple juice to cover. Blend till pureed. Combine with remaining juice in punch bowl. Add ginger ale. Serve over ice. Makes 2¾ quarts.

HOLIDAY WASSAIL

1 17-ounce can apricot halves,
    undrained
1 6-ounce can frozen pineapple juice
    concentrate
1 cup orange juice
4 cups apple juice
6 inches stick cinnamon
1 teaspoon whole cloves
¼ teaspoon whole cardamom seeds,
    crushed
  Orange slices

Put first 3 ingredients in blender container; blend till pureed. Heat with next 4 ingredients to boiling; reduce heat and simmer 15 to 20 minutes; strain. Serve in mugs with orange slice floaters. Makes about 2 quarts.

SUNSHINE PUNCH

1 3-ounce package orange-pineapple
    flavored gelatin
1 cup boiling water
1 6-ounce can frozen pineapple juice
    concentrate
1 6-ounce can frozen orange juice
    concentrate
5 cups cold water
1 28-ounce bottle ginger ale, chilled
  Ice cubes
  Orange slices

Put gelatin and 1 cup boiling water in blender container; blend at low speed till gelatin is dissolved. Add pineapple juice concentrate, orange juice concentrate, and *1 cup* of the cold water to gelatin mixture in blender container; blend till combined. Pour mixture into punch bowl; stir in remaining 4 cups cold water. Add ice cubes; carefully pour in chilled ginger ale. Float oranges. Makes 2¾ quarts.

SPICED FRUIT SPARKLE

⅔ cup sugar
1½ cups water
6 inches stick cinnamon
12 whole cloves
1 6-ounce can frozen pineapple juice
    concentrate
1 6-ounce can frozen orange juice
    concentrate
2 cups water
¼ cup lemon juice
  Ice cubes
1 28-ounce bottle ginger ale,
    chilled
  Cinnamon sticks

In medium saucepan combine first 4 ingredients. Simmer, covered, for 15 minutes; strain. Cool. Put juice concentrates, 2 cups water, and lemon juice in blender container; blend till frothy. Add to strained mixture; chill.

Before serving, pour mixture over ice cubes in punch bowl. Slowly pour ginger ale into bowl. Serve along with cinnamon stick stirrers. Makes about 2 quarts.

Blender tip: Your blender is not an ice crusher. However, many models do allow you to chop or liquefy a few ice cubes as long as (1) there is at least 1 cup of liquid in blender container and (2) ice cubes are added one by one, blending till chopped after each addition. Be sure to read manufacturer's instruction booklet on this point before using this tip for chopping ice.

CIDER FIZZ

Soda water or ginger ale give effervescence—

    2 jiggers gold label rum (3 ounces)
    ¼ cup chilled apple cider
    1 tablespoon lemon juice
    1 teaspoon sugar
    ½ cup crushed or cracked ice
      Ice cubes
      Soda water *or* ginger ale, chilled

Place rum, cider, lemon juice, sugar, and crushed ice in blender container; blend 20 seconds. Put 2 ice cubes in 2 large highball glasses. Pour blended mixture over ice cubes; fill with soda or ginger ale. Makes 2 drinks.

BACARDI COCKTAIL

Grenadine syrup lends a rosy pink color to this drink as pictured on page 65—

    2 jiggers Bacardi rum (3 ounces)
      Juice of ½ lime
    2 dashes grenadine syrup
    ½ cup crushed or cracked ice

Put all ingredients in blender container; blend quickly to mix and chill drink. Strain into old-fashioned glass. Makes 1 drink.

FROZEN DAIQUIRI

Serve a small wedge of fresh lime with this frosty drink as pictured on page 65—

    2 jiggers light rum (3 ounces)
    1 tablespoon lime
    2 tablespoons confectioners' sugar
    2 cups crushed ice

Place all ingredients in blender container. Add ingredients and blend until consistency of snow. Serve immediately with straw. Makes 1.

BEACHCOMBER COCKTAIL

    1½ jiggers light rum (2¼ ounces)
    ½ jigger Cointreau (¾ ounce)
      Juice of ½ lime
    1 teaspoon maraschino cherry syrup
    ½ cup crushed or cracked ice

Place all ingredients in blender container. Blend quickly to mix and chill drink. Pour into large cocktail glass. Makes 1 drink.

HELPFUL MEASUREMENTS

1 jigger equals 1½ ounces or 3 tablespoons
1 ounce equals 2 tablespoons
Juice of 1 lime equals about 1 tablespoon
Juice of 1 lemon equals about 3 tablespoons

The alcoholic beverages in this section are based on standard bartending proportions.

CHERRY BLOSSOM

>   5 jiggers brandy (7½ ounces)
>   4 jiggers cherry brandy (6 ounces)
>   1 tablespoon Curacao
>   1 tablespoon lemon juice
>   1 tablespoon grenadine syrup
>   1½ cups crushed or cracked ice

Place all ingredients in blender container. Blend quickly to mix and chill drink. Strain into glasses. Makes 6 drinks.

GRASSHOPPER

>   ⅔ jigger green crème de menthe
>   (1 ounce)
>   ⅔ jigger white crème de cacao
>   (1 ounce)
>   ⅔ jigger whipping cream (1 ounce)
>   ½ cup crushed or cracked ice

Place all ingredients in blender container. Blend quickly to mix and chill drink. Serve in champagne glass. Makes 1 drink.

GRASSHOPPER PUNCH

A smooth ice cream version of this favorite—

>   5 ounces green crème de menthe
>   3 ounces white crème de cacao
>   1 quart vanilla ice cream

Put liqueurs in blender. Add ice cream, a spoonful at a time, blending smooth after each addition. Serve immediately. Makes 6.

ALEXANDER

>   ⅔ jigger brandy (1 ounce)
>   ⅔ jigger crème de cacao (1 ounce)
>   ⅔ jigger whipping cream (1 ounce)
>   ½ cup crushed or cracked ice

Put all ingredients in blender container. Blend quickly to mix and chill drink. Strain the mixture into glass. Makes 1 drink.

SIDECAR

>   1 jigger brandy (1½ ounces)
>   ½ jigger Cointreau (¾ ounce)
>   ½ jigger lemon juice (¾ ounce)
>   ½ cup crushed or cracked ice

Place all ingredients in blender container. Blend quickly to mix and chill the drink. Strain into glass. Makes 1 drink.

STINGER

>   1 jigger brandy (1½ ounces)
>   1 jigger white crème de menthe
>   (1½ ounces)
>   ½ cup crushed or cracked ice

Place all ingredients in blender container. Blend quickly to mix and chill drink. Strain into glass. Makes 1 drink.

FESTIVAL COCKTAIL

>   ½ jigger apricot brandy (¾ ounce)
>   ½ jigger crème de cacao (¾ ounce)
>   ½ jigger whipping cream (¾ ounce)
>   1 teaspoon grenadine syrup
>   ½ cup crushed or cracked ice

Put apricot brandy, crème de cacao, whipping cream, and grenadine syrup with crushed ice into the blender container; blend quickly to mix well and chill the drink. Strain the mixture into glass. Makes 1 drink.

ALEXANDER'S SISTER

Use either white or green crème de menthe—

>   1 jigger dry gin (1½ onuces)
>   ½ jigger crème de menthe (¾ ounce)
>   ½ jigger whipping cream (¾ ounce)
>   ½ cup crushed or cracked ice

Put all ingredients in blender container. Blend quickly to mix and chill the drink. Strain into glass. Makes 1 drink.

RAMOZ FIZZ

The New Orleans favorite pictured on page 65—

1½ jiggers dry gin (2¼ ounces)
1 egg white
⅔ jigger whipping cream (1 ounce)
3 dashes orange flower water
Juice of ½ lime
Juice of ½ lemon
½ cup crushed or cracked ice
Soda water
Confectioners' sugar

Put gin, egg white, cream, orange flower water, lime and lemon juices, and ice in blender container. Blend quickly to mix and chill drink. Strain it into frosted glass which was prepared by rubbing the rim of the glass with the cut surface of the lemon then dipping rim in sugar. Add soda water, if desired. Makes 1.

PINK LADY

1 jigger gin (1½ ounces)
½ jigger apple brandy (¾ ounce)
1 tablespoon grenadine syrup
1 tablespoon lemon juice
1 egg white
½ cup crushed or cracked ice

Place all ingredients in blender; blend to mix. Strain into cocktail glass. Makes 1 drink.

TOM COLLINS

The long cool drink pictured on page 65—

3 tablespoons lemon juice
1 teaspoon sugar
1 jigger gin (1½ ounces)
½ cup crushed or cracked ice
Ice cubes
Soda water

Put first 4 ingredients in blender container; blend to mix and chill drink. Put 3 ice cubes in tall glass. Pour blender mixture over ice. Fill glass with soda water. Makes 1 drink.

MARGARITA

⅔ jigger tequila (1 ounce)
Dash Triple Sec
Juice of ½ lime
½ cup crushed or cracked ice

Put all ingredients in blender container; blend to mix. Strain into salt-rimmed cocktail glass prepared by rubbing glass rim with cut lime and dipping in salt. Makes 1 drink.

BLOODY MARY

1 jigger vodka (1½ ounces)
2 jiggers tomato juice (3 ounces)
⅓ jigger lemon juice (½ ounce)
Dash *each* salt, pepper, and
Worcestershire sauce
½ cup crushed or cracked ice

Place all ingredients in blender container. Blend quickly to just mix and chill drink. Strain into glass. Makes 1 drink.

APPLEJACK FLIP

As pictured on page 65—

2⅔ jiggers applejack (4 ounces)
1 egg
2 teaspoons sugar
½ cup crushed or cracked ice
Ground nutmeg

Put applejack, egg, sugar, and ice in blender container; blend to mix. Pour into 6-ounce glasses; sprinkle with nutmeg. Makes 6 drinks.

SCARLET O'HARA

1½ jiggers Southern Comfort
1½ jiggers cranberry juice (2¼ ounces)
Juice of ¼ lime
½ cup crushed or cracked ice

Place all ingredients in blender. Turn on and off to mix. Strain into glass. Makes 1 drink.

TEMPTING TIDBITS AND DIPS

When planning an elegant party menu, you'll need to turn to your blender often in preparing the fabulous dips, fillings, and other appetizer goodies. Many delicacies can be made hours ahead, while those that do require last-minute attention are easy to prepare.

STUFFED MUSHROOMS

    2 6-ounce cans mushroom crowns
    3 slices bacon
    1 thin slice of onion
    1 slice bread, torn in pieces
        Dash Worcestershire sauce
        Salt
    1 tablespoon grated Parmesan cheese

Hollow out mushrooms; reserve ¼ cup of pieces. Crisp-cook bacon; drain, reserving drippings. Cook onion in drippings till tender. Put onion, bacon, reserved mushrooms, and next 2 ingredients in blender container; blend till chopped. Sprinkle crowns with salt; pile chopped mixture in crowns. Top with cheese. Broil 3 or 4 inches from heat till hot and golden. Makes 30 appetizers.

PEPPY DEVILED EGGS

    6 hard-cooked eggs, halved
  ¼ cup mayonnaise or salad dressing
    1 teaspoon prepared mustard
        Dash pepper
    5 small pimiento-stuffed green olives*
    1 small dill pickle
        Paprika

Remove yolks from egg halves; put with next 5 ingredients in blender container. Blend till olives and pickle are finely chopped. Fill egg white halves with mixture; sprinkle with paprika. Chill well. Makes 12 appetizers.

  *Or use 2 to 3 anchovies or ½ to 1 teaspoon prepared horseradish for different flavors.

MENU

Egg-Salmon Ribbon Loaf*
Apple-Stuffed Edam*
Chili-Cheese Dip* Bacon-Blue Dip*
Assorted Crackers, Chips, Relishes
Beverages

*See index listing for page number.

PEPPERONI TARTLETS

Fill tiny pastry tartlets of piecrust mix with delectable cheese and pepperoni filling. Serve them warm to your guests—

    1 stick piecrust mix
  ½ cup milk
    2 eggs
    2 ounces sliced pepperoni
    1 ounce process American cheese,
        cut in cubes (¼ cup)
  ¼ small onion, cut in pieces
  ¼ teaspoon salt

Prepare piecrust mix according to package directions; roll pastry out thinly. With 2½-inch cutter, cut pastry into 24 circles. Fit circles inside ungreased 1¾-inch muffin pans; press dough against bottom and sides of pan. Prick pastry with fork. Bake at 450° till golden brown, about 8 to 10 minutes.

  Meanwhile put milk, eggs, sliced pepperoni, cheese cubes, onion, and salt in blender container. Adjust lid; blend ingredients till pepperoni is finely chopped.

  Remove baked tarts from oven; reduce oven temperature to 350°. Spoon pepperoni filling into tarts. Bake at 350° till knife inserted into filling comes out clean, about 10 to 12 minutes. Cool slightly; carefully remove tarts from pan. Serve warm. Makes 24 appetizers.

MARINATED SHRIMP

        1 cup salad oil
        ¼ cup white vinegar
        1½ teaspoons salt
        1 small clove garlic
           Dash bottled hot pepper sauce
        1 teaspoon paprika
        1 stalk celery, sliced
        2 sprigs parsley
        ½ green pepper, cut in pieces
        2 green onions with tops, sliced
        1 pound shelled cooked shrimp

Put salad oil, white vinegar, salt, garlic, bottled hot pepper sauce, and paprika in blender container; blend till mixture is combined. Add celery, parsley, green pepper, and green onion to mixture in blender container; blend till finely chopped. Pour marinade mixture over shrimp in bowl. Cover; marinate in refrigerator 24 hours, spooning marinade over shrimp occasionally. Serve on picks.

QUICHE WEDGES

        Piecrust mix for one 8-inch
           pie shell
        3 eggs
        1 10-ounce package frozen Welsh
           rarebit, partially thawed
        ⅛ teaspoon pepper
        5 slices bacon, crisp-cooked and
           drained
           Pimiento stars
           Parsley sprigs

Prepare pie shell according to package directions. Bake; cool. Put eggs in blender container; blend till foamy. Break Welsh rarebit in pieces into blender container; add pepper. Blend till combined. Add bacon to blender container; blend till coarsely chopped. Pour into pie shell. Bake at 350° till knife inserted off-center comes out clean, about 40 minutes.

Let stand at room temperature for 10 to 15 minutes before serving. With knife, cut into small wedges to serve. Top each piece with a pimiento star, if desired. Garnish with fresh parsley sprigs. Makes 12 appetizers.

APPLE-STUFFED EDAM

Stuff red Edam shell with apple-cheese mixture—

        8 ounces Edam *or* Gouda cheese
        1 medium apple, cut in eighths
           and cored
        ½ cup milk
        1 teaspoon lemon juice
           Dash salt

Cut top off cheese. Carefully remove cheese from shell. Cut cheese in cubes; set aside. Put apple, milk, lemon juice, and salt in blender container; blend till finely chopped. Add cheese cubes, a few at a time, to mixture in blender container; blend till nearly smooth. (When necessary, stop blender and use rubber spatula to scrape down sides.)

Spoon into cheese shell. Chill. Chill any extra mixture separately and use to replenish red shell. Serve with assorted crackers.

Glamorize your buffet table with easy Quiche Wedges made with packaged, frozen Welsh rarebit and crisp-cooked bacon.

THREE-CHEESE MOLD

   2 tablespoons cold water
1½ teaspoons unflavored gelatin
   2 tablespoons boiling water
   3 ounces sharp natural Cheddar cheese,
      cut in cubes (¾ cup)
   ½ cup cream-style cottage cheese
   1 ounce blue cheese, crumbled (¼ cup)
   ¼ cup dairy sour cream
   1 thin slice of onion
   2 sprigs parsley
   ½ teaspoon Worcestershire sauce
      Parsley

Put cold water and gelatin in blender container; let stand a few minutes to soften. Add boiling water; blend till gelatin is dissolved. Add Cheddar cheese, cottage cheese, blue cheese, sour cream, onion, 2 sprigs parsley, and Worcestershire sauce to mixture in blender container; blend till smooth. (If necessary, stop blender and use rubber spatula to scrape down sides of container.) Pack into a 1½-cup mold; chill. Unmold; garnish with additional parsley. Serve with assorted crackers.

SHERRIED CHEESE BALLS

   8 ounces sharp natural Cheddar
      cheese, cut in cubes (2 cups)
   2 tablespoons butter or margarine,
      softened
   ½ teaspoon dry mustard
   ⅓ cup dry sherry
   3 tablespoons milk
   ½ cup stemmed parsley sprigs, packed
   2 tablespoons sesame seeds, toasted
      Paprika

Put *half* the cheese in blender container; blend till chopped. Remove and set aside. Repeat with remaining cheese. Put cheese, butter or margarine, dry mustard, dry sherry, and milk in blender container; blend till smooth. Chill; divide into thirds. Form each into a ball.

Put parsley in blender container; blend till chopped. Roll one ball in chopped parsley, another in toasted sesame seed, and the third in paprika. Serve with assorted crackers.

CORNED BEEF PÂTÉ

   1 12-ounce can corned beef
   1 8-ounce package cream cheese,
      cut in cubes and softened
   1 6-ounce can mushrooms, drained
   ¼ cup milk
   1 envelope green onion dip mix
   2 sprigs parsley

Break beef into chunks; put ⅓ in blender container. Blend till chopped; put in bowl. Repeat with remaining beef. Put remaining ingredients in blender container; blend smooth. Combine with beef; mix well. Mold in small bowl; chill. Unmold. Serve with crackers.

SNOW-CAPPED PÂTÉ

   ½ cup chopped onion
   1 small clove garlic, crushed
   ¼ cup butter or margarine
   1 pound fresh or frozen chicken
      livers, thawed
   2 teaspoons all-purpose flour
   ¼ teaspoon salt
   ¼ teaspoon dried thyme leaves,
      crushed
      Dash pepper
   2 tablespoons dry sherry
   2 3-ounce packages cream cheese,
      cut in cubes and softened
   3 tablespoons milk
   ½ cup stemmed parsley sprigs, packed
   ½ cup pecans

Cook onion and garlic in butter till tender. Add livers; cook, covered, over low heat till no longer pink, about 7 to 8 minutes. Stir in flour, salt, thyme, and pepper. Add sherry; cook and stir 1 minute. Transfer to blender container; blend till smooth. (When necessary, use rubber spatula to scrape down sides of container.) Mold in small greased bowl; chill.

Unmold. Add cream cheese and milk to blender container; blend smooth. Spread cream cheese mixture over mold. Chill till serving time. Put parsley and pecans in blender container; blend till chopped. Sprinkle atop pâté. Chill. Serve with assorted crackers.

BACON-BLUE DIP

½ cup dairy sour cream
1 3-ounce package cream cheese, cut
   in cubes and softened
2 ounces blue cheese, crumbled (½ cup)
1 tablespoon instant minced onion
4 strips bacon, crisp-cooked, drained,
   and crumbled
1 large green pepper, top and seeds
   removed

Put first 4 ingredients in blender container; blend till mixture is smooth. Chill. Before serving, stir in crumbled bacon. Serve mixture in green pepper, if desired. Makes about 1 cup.

DEVILED DIP

1 5-ounce jar pimiento cheese spread
1 4½-ounce can deviled ham
¼ cup mayonnaise or salad dressing
1 tablespoon dried parsley flakes
1 thin slice of onion
4 or 5 drops bottled hot pepper sauce
1 large green pepper, top and seeds
   removed

Put cheese spread, deviled ham, mayonnaise, parsley flakes, onion, and hot pepper sauce in blender container; blend smooth. Chill. Serve in green pepper, if desired. Serve with corn chips and vegetable dippers. Makes 1 cup.

Remove the tops and seeds from big green peppers
to use as interesting bowls for dip and fill with creamy
Spaghetti Dip, Bacon-Blue Dip, and Deviled Dip.

SPAGHETTI DIP

    1 large green pepper
    1 cup dairy sour cream
    2 tablespoons dry spaghetti sauce mix

Remove top and seeds from green pepper. Remove stem from green pepper top; discard. Place green pepper top and all the remaining ingredients in blender container; blend till green pepper is coarsely chopped. Chill well. Fill green pepper with dip. Makes about 1 cup.

GUACAMOLE

    2 tablespoons lemon juice
    ¾ teaspoon salt
    1 small tomato, peeled and cut in
       pieces
    ¼ medium onion
    2 to 3 canned green chilies, seeded
    2 ripe avocados, halved, seeded,
       peeled, and cut in cubes

Put all ingredients in blender container. Blend ingredients till smooth. (When necessary, stop blender and use rubber spatula to scrape down sides of container.) Makes 2 cups.
Special cooking tip: For a more colorful dip, reserve half the tomato; add tomato at end and blend only till tomato is coarsely chopped.

SHRIMP COCKTAIL DIP

    1 8-ounce package cream cheese,
       cut in cubes and softened
    1 cup chili sauce
 1½ tablespoons lemon juice
    1 tablespoon prepared horseradish
    2 teaspoons Worcestershire sauce
    ½ teaspoon salt
      Shelled cooked shrimp, chilled

Put all ingredients, except shrimp, in blender container. Adjust lid; blend till mixed. (When necessary, stop blender and use rubber spatula to scrape down sides.) Pour mixture into small bowl; chill thoroughly. Serve with chilled shrimp. Makes about 2 cups.

AVOCADO-CRAB DIP

    1 large avocado, halved, seeded,
       peeled, and cut in cubes
    1 tablespoon lemon juice
    1 thin slice of onion
    1 teaspoon Worcestershire sauce
    1 8-ounce package cream cheese,
       cut in cubes and softened
    ¼ cup dairy sour cream
    ¼ teaspoon salt
    1 7½-ounce can crab meat, drained,
       flaked, and cartilage removed

Put avocado, lemon juice, onion, and Worcestershire sauce in blender container; blend till smooth. Add cream cheese, dairy sour cream, and salt to mixture in blender container; blend till combined. Stir in crab meat; chill well. Serve with assorted crackers.

WINE-CHEESE DIP

    ¼ cup tawny port *or* sauterne
    1 8-ounce package cream cheese, cut
       in cubes and softened
    2 ounces blue cheese, crumbled
       (¼ cup)
      Dash garlic salt

Put tawny port *or* sauterne, cream cheese, blue cheese, and dash garlic salt in blender container; blend till mixture is smooth. Serve with assorted crackers. Makes 1⅓ cups.

CREAMY CLAM DIP

    1 7½-ounce can minced clams,
       undrained
    1 8-ounce package cream cheese, cut
       in cubes and softened
    1 green onion with top, sliced

Drain minced clams; reserve 3 tablespoons of the clam liquid. Set aside. Put cream cheese, reserved clam liquid, and green onion in blender container; blend till mixture is smooth. Add drained clams to cheese mixture in blender container; blend till mixed. Makes 1½ cups.

HAM SALAD SPREAD

½ cup mayonnaise or salad dressing
1 large sweet pickle
1 small stalk celery, sliced
½ teaspoon prepared mustard
1½ cups cubed, fully cooked ham
    Butter or margarine, softened
2 dozen 2-inch bread rounds, cut from
    thinly sliced bread
    Parsley

Put mayonnaise or salad dressing, sweet pickle, celery, and prepared mustard in blender container; blend till pickle and celery are chopped. Add ham pieces, about ½ cup at a time, to mixture in blender container. Blend till ham is chopped. Chill. Makes 1⅔ cups.

Lightly butter bread rounds; spread about 1 tablespoon of the ham mixture on each bread round. Garnish with parsley, if desired. *Special cooking tip:* If desired, toast bread rounds on one side under broiler. Spread untoasted side with ham mixture. Broil 3 to 4 inches from heat till heated, 1 to 2 minutes.

PARTY REUBENS

½ 12-ounce can corned beef, cut
    in pieces
1 8-ounce can sauerkraut, drained
½ cup Thousand Island salad dressing
30 slices party rye bread
2 ounces process Swiss cheese, torn
    in pieces (½ cup)

Place *half* the corned beef in blender container; blend till chopped. Remove chopped meat to bowl; repeat with remaining corned beef. Put drained sauerkraut and Thousand Island salad dressing in blender container; blend till sauerkraut is chopped and mixture is blended. Combine with corned beef in bowl.

Lightly toast one side of rye bread under broiler, about 3 to 4 inches from heat. Spread corned beef mixture on untoasted sides of rye bread. Top each sandwich with Swiss cheese. Broil 3 to 4 inches from heat till cheese melts and corned beef is heated through, about 1 to 2 minutes. Makes 30 appetizer sandwiches.

SALMON SPREAD

¼ cup mayonnaise or salad dressing
1 teaspoon lemon juice
1 7¾-ounce can salmon, drained
¼ cup pitted ripe olives
½ stalk celery, sliced
½ teaspoon prepared horseradish

Put ingredients in blender; blend till olives and celery are chopped. Makes 1 cup.

EGG SALAD SPREAD

¼ cup mayonnaise or salad dressing
4 hard-cooked eggs, quartered
1 large sweet pickle
½ teaspoon celery salt
1 slice canned pimiento

Put ingredients, except pimiento, in blender container; blend till mixture is combined. Add pimiento; blend till chopped. Makes 1 cup.

EGG-SALMON RIBBON LOAF

1 loaf unsliced white sandwich bread
    Butter or margarine, softened
1 cup Salmon Spread
1 tomato, peeled and thinly sliced
1 cup Egg Salad Spread
⅓ cup milk
4 3-ounce packages cream cheese,
    cut in cubes and softened

• • •

    Parsley
    Radish slices

Trim crusts from bread; slice lengthwise into 4 layers. Butter layers. Spread first layer with Salmon Spread; arrange tomato slices on second layer and spread Egg Salad Spread on third layer. Assemble loaf, using 2 spatulas to support layers. Wrap in foil; chill well.

Pour milk into blender container. With blender slowly running, add cream cheese cubes gradually. Blend till fluffy. Frost loaf with mixture. Chill till firm. Garnish with parsley and radish slices. Makes 10 slices.

Coping with calories, leftovers, baby foods, and special diets, or changing seasonal fruits and produce into jams and relishes are among the extra duties a blender does best.

Subtract calories from appetizing dips, flavorful salad dressings, and desserts by substituting blender-whipped foods for ingredients with a higher calorie count.

Consider leftovers in light of the sophisticated main dishes or tasty sandwiches they can become. Save money by pureeing cooked foods in small amounts to suit infant needs or those of a family member following a smooth diet.

Try your hand at making winter preserves and summer relishes. Pack some for family use, but remember their gift-giving possibilities, too.

Utilize leftover chicken in this special Chicken Curry dish to be served over rice and topped with Indian Chutney, chopped peanuts, or coconut.

Blender specialties

CALORIE-CUTTING KNOW-HOW

Discover the blender as a calorie-trimming tool in meal planning. With ingredient substitution and the use of your imagination you can turn out a finished appetizer, main dish, salad dressing, or dessert that has all the good flavor of the original recipe, but fewer of the calories that were there.

Use the blender to reconstitute nonfat dry milk, the weight- and budget-watcher's friend. You'll be pleased at the full flavor of the milk when served as a low-calorie, highly nutritious beverage. Also, a spin in the blender transforms an envelope of powdered diet food and cold milk into a frothy, satisfying milk shake of your favorite flavor.

MENU

(507 calories)
Vegetable Meat Loaf*
Baked Potato
Cottage Cheese Topper*
Lettuce Wedge   Tomato Dressing*
Café Au Lait Cheesecake*
Beverage

*See index listing for page number.

VEGETABLE MEAT LOAF

    1 medium carrot, sliced
    ⅛ small onion, cut in pieces
    ¼ medium green pepper, cut in pieces
    1 stalk celery, sliced
    1 tomato, peeled and cut up
    ¼ teaspoon salt
    2 slices bread, torn in pieces
    1 egg
    ¾ teaspoon salt
    ½ teaspoon Worcestershire sauce
    1 pound lean ground beef

Put first 4 ingredients in blender container; blend till coarsely chopped. In saucepan combine chopped vegetables, tomato, and ¼ teaspoon salt. Simmer, covered, till vegetables are crisp-tender, about 7 to 8 minutes. Drain.

Put bread, egg, ¾ teaspoon salt, and Worcestershire in blender container; blend smooth. Transfer to bowl; add beef. Mix well. Pat into a 10x8-inch rectangle on waxed paper. Spread vegetable mixture over meat, leaving 1-inch margin. Roll jelly-roll fashion, beginning with narrow side. Seal sides, seams, and ends. Place roll, seam side down, in baking dish. Bake at 350° for 50 minutes. Serves 5. (215 calories/serving.)

APPLE-STUFFED BASS

    2 apples, peeled, cored, and cut up
    ½ small onion, cut in pieces
    2 sprigs parsley
    1 tablespoon butter or margarine
    ½ teaspoon salt
    1½ cups herb-seasoned stuffing cubes
    2 tablespoons butter, melted
    2 tablespoons lemon juice
    1 4-pound dressed striped bass

Put apple, onion, and parsley in blender container; cover with *cold* water. Blend till chopped; drain. Put apple mixture, 1 tablespoon butter, and ½ teaspoon salt in saucepan; simmer 10 minutes. Toss with seasoned stuffing cubes. Combine melted butter and lemon juice; brush fish cavity with mixture. Salt lightly. Spoon stuffing into cavity; brush fish with butter. Cover. Bake at 350° for 50 to 60 minutes. Serves 10. (166 calories/serving.)

Coffee and cream flavor

Create your own design with zwieback→ crumbs atop Café Au Lait Cheesecake. Cottage cheese replaces cream cheese.

SPICED ICED COFFEE

1½ cups cold skim milk
2 tablespoons sugar
2 tablespoons instant coffee powder
¼ teaspoon ground cinnamon

• • •

1 16-ounce bottle low-calorie cola
   beverage, chilled

Put milk, sugar, instant coffee powder, and ground cinnamon in blender container; blend till combined. Just before serving, carefully add chilled low-calorie cola beverage. Stir gently with an up-and-down motion. Serve over ice. Serves 6. (62 calories/serving.)

Enjoy cutting calories in your diet with such beverages as Banana Milk Shake or Spiced Iced Coffee made in the blender.

BANANA MILK SHAKE

1 medium-large banana
1 cup cold skim milk
½ teaspoon vanilla

Peel banana; cut into 1-inch pieces. Wrap in foil; freeze. Put milk, vanilla, and frozen banana pieces in blender container; blend till smooth. Serves 2. (95 calories/serving.)

SLIM-JIM FRAPPÉ

1 envelope vanilla-flavored powdered
   diet food
1 cup cold skim milk
1 egg
¼ teaspoon rum flavoring
   Ground nutmeg

Put all ingredients, except nutmeg, in blender container; blend till combined. Pour into 3-cup freezer tray. Freeze till almost firm. Spoon into blender container; blend till crushed. Serve in sherbet glasses; sprinkle with nutmeg. Serves 2. (116 calories/serving.)

VANILLA-FRUIT STARTER

1 envelope vanilla-flavored powdered
   diet food
1 cup cold skim milk
⅛ teaspoon ground mace
1 fresh peach, peeled *or* 2 canned
   peach halves, juice pack

Put ingredients in blender container; blend till combined. Serves 1. (179 calories/serving.)

INSTANT MOCHA

1 envelope chocolate-flavored
   powdered diet food
1 cup cold skim milk
1½ teaspoons instant coffee powder

Put ingredients in blender container; blend till combined. Serves 1. (149 calories/serving.)

LOW-CALORIE DIP

1 12-ounce carton cream-style cottage
  cheese (1½ cups)
1 tablespoon low-calorie mayonnaise-
  type dressing
1 teaspoon mixed salad herbs
  Snipped parsley

Put first 3 ingredients in blender container;
blend till almost smooth. Chill. Top with parsley. Makes 1½ cups. (16 calories/tablespoon.)

TOMATO DRESSING

1 8-ounce can tomatoes
2 tablespoons vinegar
1 tablespoon salad oil
1 thin slice of small onion
¼ small green pepper, cut in pieces
1 sprig parsley
1 teaspoon sugar
½ teaspoon salt
¼ teaspoon chili powder
  Dash pepper
  Few drops bottled hot pepper sauce
  Few drops red food coloring

Blend all ingredients in blender container till
vegetables are chopped. Chill. Shake before using. Makes 1¼ cups. (10 calories/tablespoon.)

STRAWBERRY SHERBET

1 3-ounce package strawberry-flavored
  gelatin
1 cup boiling water
¾ cup cold water
1 tablespoon lemon juice
  Dash ground cinnamon
1 16-ounce package frozen strawberries,
  partially thawed

Blend first 2 ingredients at low speed in blender till dissolved. Add rest of ingredients to
blender container; blend till mixed. Freeze in
two 4-cup freezer trays. Break into chunks.
Beat smooth in chilled bowl. Return to trays;
freeze. Serves 8. (102 calories/serving.)

COTTAGE CHEESE TOPPER

1 cup cream-style cottage cheese
1 tablespoon lemon juice
3 to 4 tablespoons water
1 tablespoon snipped chives

Put first 2 ingredients in blender. Slowly add
water, blending till desired consistency. Add
chives. Serve over baked potatoes. Makes 1
cup. (15 calories/tablespoon.)

CAFÉ AU LAIT CHEESECAKE

6 zwieback
½ teaspoon ground cinnamon
¼ cup cold water
2 envelopes unflavored gelatin
½ cup boiling water
¾ cup brown sugar
¼ teaspoon salt
3 cups cream-style cottage cheese
2 egg yolks
4 teaspoons instant coffee powder
1 teaspoon vanilla
2 egg whites
¼ teaspoon cream of tartar
1 14½-ounce can evaporated skim
  milk, chilled icy cold (1¾ cups)

Break zwieback into blender container; add
cinnamon. Blend to crumbs. Remove and set
aside. Put cold water and gelatin in blender
container; let stand a few minutes to soften.
Add boiling water, brown sugar, and salt to
container; blend till dissolved. Add cottage
cheese, egg yolks, coffee powder, and vanilla
to blender; blend smooth. Pour into bowl.

Beat egg whites with cream of tartar till
stiff peaks form. Whip evaporated milk till
soft peaks form. Fold whipped evaporated
milk into gelatin mixture; fold in egg whites.
Pour into 8- or 9-inch springform pan. Sprinkle crumbs over cake. Chill; remove sides of
pan. Serves 12. (170 calories/serving.)
Special cooking tip: To make design, cut pattern from heavy paper. Insert 2 straight pins
in pattern and center on cake, pin points up.
Sprinkle crumbs around pattern; remove pattern and pins by grasping pins.

FAMILY-PLEASING LEFTOVERS

How to turn yesterday's roast into tomorrow's dinner is a constant problem. The solution is to chop those odd-sized pieces in your blender and use them in exotic curries, spicy sauces, and imaginative sandwiches.

SPEEDY STROGANOFF LOAF

    4 ounces sharp natural Cheddar
        cheese, cut in cubes (1 cup)
    ¼ small onion
    2 tablespoons butter or margarine
    2 cups cubed, cooked roast beef
    8 medium, pitted ripe olives
    1 envelope stroganoff seasoning mix
    1 cup water
    ½ cup dairy sour cream
            • • •
    1 unsliced loaf Vienna bread
        Butter or margarine, softened
        Green pepper rings
        Cherry tomatoes, halved

Put cheese in blender container; blend till chopped. Remove and set aside. Put onion in blender container; blend till chopped. In medium saucepan cook onion in butter or margarine till tender but not browned. Meanwhile, place about *half* of the roast beef at a time in blender; blend till chopped. Remove.

Put pitted ripe olives in blender container; blend till coarsely chopped. Stir stroganoff seasoning mix into onion in saucepan; gradually blend in water. Add chopped beef and olives to mixture in saucepan. Cover and simmer for 8 to 10 minutes, stirring occasionally. Stir in sour cream; heat through over low heat.

Cut Vienna bread in half lengthwise. Toast under broiler till golden brown; spread cut surfaces with softened butter or margarine. Spread *half* of the meat mixture on each half of bread; arrange green pepper rings alternately with tomato halves atop. Sprinkle with cheese. Place on baking sheet and bake at 375° for 7 to 10 minutes. Serves 8 to 10.

MENU

Chicken Curry*   Hot Rice
Indian Chutney*
Chopped Peanuts   Shredded Coconut
Whole Wheat Rolls   Butter
Fruit Compote
Beverage

*See index listing for page number.

HAM FIESTA ROLLS

    1½ cups cubed, fully cooked ham
    6-8 large hard rolls
      4 ounces process American cheese,
          cut in cubes (1 cup)
      2 green onions, sliced
      8 small, pimiento-stuffed green olives
      1 hard-cooked egg, quartered
      ¼ cup chili sauce
      ¼ cup mayonnaise or salad dressing
          Pimiento-stuffed green olives

Put ⅓ of the ham in blender container; blend till coarsely chopped. Remove. Repeat. Slice tops off rolls. Scoop out centers; add crumbs to cheese and onion in blender. Blend till chopped. Combine with ham. Put olives and egg in blender; blend till chopped. Add to ham and cheese. Stir in chili sauce and mayonnaise. Spoon into buns; wrap in foil. Heat at 400° for 20 to 25 minutes. Slice olives; garnish sandwiches. Serves 6 to 8.

Sandwich gallery

Use leftovers to make Speedy Stroganoff →
Loaf, Paul Revere Sandwiches, or Ham Fiesta Rolls. Serve sandwiches hot.

PAUL REVERE SANDWICHES

1 cup cubed, cooked roast pork,
  chicken, *or* turkey
1 slice of onion
⅓ cup mayonnaise or salad dressing
1 teaspoon prepared mustard
¼ teaspoon salt
1 package refrigerated biscuits
  (10 biscuits)
1 medium dill pickle, sliced in 10
  slices
  Parsley

Put meat, onion, mayonnaise or salad dressing, prepared mustard, and salt in blender container; blend till meat is chopped. (When necessary, stop blender and use rubber spatula to scrape down sides. On floured surface, roll each biscuit to a 4-inch circle.

Place a rounded tablespoon of the meat mixture in center of each biscuit circle; top with pickle slice. Fold up 3 sides of biscuit and pinch edges together to seal. Place biscuits on lightly greased baking sheet; bake at 425° till golden brown, about 8 to 10 minutes. Garnish with parsley. Serve warm. Makes 10.

CHICKEN-CHEESE CASSEROLE

4 cups corn chips
½ cup milk
1 10½-ounce can condensed cream of
  chicken soup
1 8-ounce jar process cheese spread
2 canned green chilies
2 teaspoons instant minced onion
2 cups cubed, cooked chicken

Put about *half* the corn chips in blender container; blend till coarsely crushed. Remove from blender to 1½-quart casserole. Repeat with remaining chips; remove and set aside.

Put milk, soup, cheese spread, chilies, and onion in blender container; blend till combined. Add chicken to mixture in blender container; blend till coarsely chopped. Pour soup mixture over corn chips in casserole; sprinkle with reserved chips. Bake at 350° for 35 to 40 minutes. Let stand 5 minutes. Serves 4 to 5.

HOLLANDAISE TURKEY ROAST

6 slices *or* 3 cups cubed, cooked
  turkey
1 chicken bouillon cube
½ cup hot water
½ cup milk
3 tablespoons melted butter
¼ cup all-purpose flour
¼ teaspoon salt
1 3-ounce can mushrooms, drained
2 egg yolks
¼ teaspoon salt
  Dash pepper
1 tablespoon lemon juice
¼ cup butter or margarine, melted

Put turkey in 10x6x1¾-inch baking dish. Put bouillon and water in blender; blend till dissolved. Add next 4 ingredients to blender; blend to combine. In saucepan cook and stir till thick and bubbly. Add mushrooms. Pour sauce over turkey. Bake at 350° about 15 minutes. Put next 4 ingredients in blender; blend till thick and lemon-colored. With blender at low speed, slowly add butter. Pour over turkey; broil till golden. Serves 6.

TURKEY HASH, OVEN-STYLE

8 rich round cheese crackers
1 tablespoon butter, melted
1½ cups cubed, cooked turkey
1 cup diced, cooked potatoes
1 6-ounce can evaporated milk
2 sprigs parsley
1 thin slice of onion
½ slice canned pimiento
½ teaspoon Worcestershire sauce
¼ teaspoon salt
  Dash pepper

Put crackers in blender container; blend till coarsely chopped. Toss with butter; set aside. Put *half* of turkey in blender; blend till chopped. Empty into bowl. Repeat. Toss with potatoes. Put remaining ingredients in blender; blend till chopped. Add to turkey. Turn into 1-quart casserole; add crumbs. Bake, uncovered, at 350° for 30 minutes. Serves 4.

CHICKEN CROQUETTES

½ cup chicken broth
¼ cup milk
¼ cup all-purpose flour
3 tablespoons butter or margarine
1 thin slice of small onion
1 sprig parsley
1 teaspoon lemon juice
¼ teaspoon salt
  Dash *each* pepper and paprika
1½ cups cubed, cooked chicken
2 or 3 slices dry bread
1 egg
2 tablespoons water
  Fat for frying

Put first 7 ingredients and seasonings in blender; blend till onion and parsley are finely chopped. In saucepan, cook and stir till thick and bubbly. Cook and stir 1 minute. Cool.

Put *half* the chicken in blender container; blend till finely chopped. Remove. Repeat with rest of chicken. Add to sauce; chill.

Break bread in blender container; blend to fine crumbs. With wet hands, shape chicken mixture into 8 balls. Roll in dry bread crumbs. Shape balls into cones. Dip into mixture of egg and water; roll in crumbs. Fry in deep fat (365°) 2½ to 3 minutes. Drain. Serves 4.

BLENDER BARBECUE BEEF

2 cups cubed, cooked roast beef
1 12-ounce bottle chili sauce
1 8-ounce can tomato sauce
1 thin slice of onion
½ small green pepper, cut in pieces
1 tablespoon Worcestershire sauce
1 teaspoon prepared mustard
  Dash bottled hot pepper sauce
¼ teaspoon salt
8 hamburger buns, toasted

Put *half* the beef in blender container; blend till chopped. Remove. Repeat with remaining beef. Put next 8 ingredients in blender container; blend till chopped. Combine with beef. Simmer in covered saucepan for 15 to 20 minutes. Spoon on buns. Makes 8 sandwiches.

CHICKEN CURRY

1 cup chicken broth
2 cups cubed, cooked chicken
½ medium onion, cut in pieces
4 tablespoons butter or margarine
3 to 4 teaspoons curry powder
3 tablespoons all-purpose flour
¼ teaspoon salt
  Dash pepper
1 medium tomato, peeled and quartered
  Hot cooked rice
  Curry Condiments—Indian Chutney
  (*see page 90*), chopped peanuts,
  shredded coconut

Put broth, chicken, and onion in blender container; blend till coarsely chopped. In skillet melt butter. Add curry; heat through. Stir in flour, salt, and pepper. Add chicken mixture; cook and stir till thick and bubbly.

Put tomato in blender; blend till chopped. Fold into curry mixture. Heat to boiling. Serve over rice. Pass condiments. Serves 4.

SPAGHETTI AND BEEF SAUCE

1 28-ounce can tomatoes
1 6-ounce can tomato paste
½ small onion, cut in pieces
½ medium green pepper, cut in pieces
1 clove garlic
2 teaspoons sugar
1 teaspoon salt
½ teaspoon chili powder
½ teaspoon dried oregano leaves, crushed
½ teaspoon dried basil leaves, crushed
⅛ teaspoon pepper
2 cups cubed, cooked roast beef
  Hot cooked spaghetti
  Parmesan cheese

Put first 11 ingredients in blender container; blend till chopped. Pour *half* the mixture into saucepan. Add beef to blender container; blend till chopped. Add to saucepan. Bring to boil; reduce heat and simmer 15 minutes. Serve on spaghetti; pass cheese. Serves 6.

MONEY-SAVING BABY FOODS

Using the blender to prepare food for the youngest member of the household saves mother's precious time as well as money. Small amounts of many canned or cooked foods that are part of family meals can be whirled to a smooth and creamy texture for the tiny folks to enjoy, too.

VEGETABLE MEAT COMBO

½ cup cubed, cooked lamb, beef, veal,
   or ham
½ cup cooked vegetables
¼ to ½ cup milk

Place meat, vegetables, and ¼ *cup* of the milk in blender container; blend till smooth. (If necessary, stop blender and use rubber spatula to scrape down sides of container.) Add more milk as needed to give desired consistency. Heat before serving. Makes 1 cup.

BABY'S VEGETABLES

2 tablespoons vegetable liquid, milk,
   or formula
½ cup cooked vegetables

Put all ingredients in blender container. (Or put all ingredients into small standard half-pint jar and screw on cutting assembly.) Blend till vegetables are smooth. Makes ½ cup.

BABY'S FRUIT

¾ cup cooked *or* canned fruit
2 teaspoons fruit syrup *or* water
½ teaspoon sugar

Put all ingredients in blender container. (Or put all ingredients into small standard half-pint jar and screw on cutting assembly.) Blend till fruit is smooth. Makes about ¾ cup.

Blender tip: Process small amounts of food by putting all ingredients into standard half-pint jar or small jar designed to fit on some blenders. Screw on cutting assembly and blend. Store the food in the jars.

FRUIT PUDDING

3 medium canned pear halves *or* 3
   medium canned peach halves
2 egg yolks
½ cup milk
   Fruit syrup plus water to equal
   1 cup
1 tablespoon cornstarch

Put fruit and egg yolks in blender container; blend till pureed. Add milk, fruit syrup, and cornstarch to mixture in blender container; blend till combined. Pour into saucepan; cook and stir till thick and bubbly. Makes 1½ cups.

SPECIAL DIET HELPS

Following a smooth diet for medical or dental reasons is easier to do at home with the aid of a blender. Because so many different foods can be pureed, flavor combinations need not be monotonous even though the textures are all the same.

Emphasis in these recipes is on high-protein foods that have a minimum of seasonings. However, if the special diet permits, add seasonings to taste to the baby foods on the opposite page to increase the variety of foods that can be served throughout the day.

BANANA-RASPBERRY FLIP

1 medium banana, cut in pieces
1 8-ounce carton raspberry-flavored
   yogurt
1 tablespoon sugar
4 ice cubes
  Ice cubes

Place banana pieces, yogurt, and sugar in blender container; blend till smooth. Add the 4 ice cubes, one at a time, blending after each addition till cube is chopped (*see tip, page 69*). Chill beverage, if desired, or serve over additional ice cubes. Makes 2 servings.

CREAM OF VEGETABLE SOUP

2 cups milk
2 cups cooked vegetables*
3 tablespoons butter or margarine
1 tablespoon all-purpose flour
1 teaspoon instant minced onion
1 teaspoon salt

Put all ingredients in blender container; blend till smooth. Pour mixture into saucepan. Cook over medium heat, stirring occasionally, till mixture thickens and bubbles. Simmer 1 minute longer. Makes 3 to 4 servings.
*Use cut asparagus, cut broccoli, or carrots.

CHICKEN TIMBALE

½ cup chicken broth
3 eggs
1 3-ounce can mushrooms, drained
1 sprig parsley
1 slice dry bread, torn in pieces
1 cup cubed, cooked chicken

Put all ingredients in blender container; blend till smooth. (When necessary, stop blender and use rubber spatula to scrape down sides.)

Pour into four 5- or 6-ounce greased custard cups; set in shallow pan on oven rack. Pour hot water in pan, 1 inch deep. Bake at 325° till set, 45 to 50 minutes. Makes 4 servings.

COTTAGE CHEESE CUSTARD

½ cup cream-style cottage cheese
2 tablespoons honey
¼ teaspoon vanilla
2 eggs
  Milk
  Ground nutmeg

Put first 4 ingredients in blender with cup markings or a 2 cup measuring cup; pour in milk to the 2 cup mark. Put in blender; blend smooth. Pour into four or five greased 5- or 6-ounce custard cups; set in shallow pan on oven rack. Pour hot water into pan, 1 inch deep. Top with nutmeg. Bake at 325° till set, about 40 to 50 minutes. Chill. Serves 4 or 5.

CREAMY PEACH DESSERT

⅓ cup cream-style cottage cheese
1 8¾-ounce can peaches, drained *or*
   1 fresh peach, peeled and sliced
   Dash ground nutmeg

Put ingredients in blender container; blend till smooth. Makes about ¾ cup.

JAM AND RELISH JAMBOREE

Brighten family meals by offering zippy home-made relish or spicy chutney with the meat course and by serving homemade marmalade made in your own kitchen with the breakfast toast. All the tedious cutting and chopping chores usually associated with these flavorful accompaniments are quickly taken over by the ever-so-versatile blender.

Although family enjoyment comes first, re-member that a gaily wrapped jar of jam or relish says a special thank you to a helpful neighbor or makes a thoughtful gift at holi-day, anniversary, or birthday time.

INDIAN CHUTNEY

¾ cup cider vinegar
¼ cup water
1 clove garlic
2 teaspoons curry powder
1 teaspoon salt
1 teaspoon ground ginger
¼ teaspoon ground cloves
¼ teaspoon ground cinnamon
4 green apples, peeled, cut in eighths, and cored
2 medium onions, cut in pieces
2 ounces candied citron (¼ cup)
1 cup seedless raisins
½ cup brown sugar

Put vinegar, water, garlic, curry powder, salt, ginger, cloves, and cinnamon in blender con-tainer; blend till garlic is finely chopped. Add *half* the apples and *half* the onions to mixture in blender container; blend till coarsely chopped. (When necessary stop blender and use rubber spatula to scrape down sides.)

Add remaining apple and onions, citron, raisins, and brown sugar to mixture in blender container; blend till coarsely chopped. Pour into saucepan and simmer, uncovered, over low heat about 45 minutes to 1 hour, stirring occasionally to prevent sticking. Seal in hot, scalded jars. Makes six ½-pint jars.

FRESH TOMATO RELISH

½ medium onion, cut in pieces
½ medium green pepper, cut in pieces
¼ cup vinegar
2 teaspoons sugar
1 teaspoon celery seed
½ teaspoon salt
Dash pepper
2 medium tomatoes, cut up

Put onion, green pepper, vinegar, sugar, cel-ery seed, salt, and pepper in blender container; blend till onion and green pepper are coarsely chopped. Add tomatoes; blend till chopped. Chill. Drain before serving. Makes 1¼ cups.

ORANGE MARMALADE

4 medium oranges
1 medium lemon
1½ cups water
¼ teaspoon baking soda
6 cups sugar
½ of a 6-ounce bottled liquid fruit pectin

Remove peel from oranges and lemon; scrape off excess white membrane. Put *half* the peel and *half* the water in blender container; blend till peel is finely chopped. Pour water and chopped peel in large saucepan. Repeat pro-cess for remaining peel and water. Add baking soda to mixture in saucepan; bring to boiling. Reduce heat; cover. Cook 10 minutes.

Meanwhile, quarter fruit and remove seeds. Put fruit in blender container; blend till pureed. Add to orange peel mixture in sauce-pan; cover and cook slowly for 20 minutes.

Measure mixture (should be about 3 cups) into large kettle or Dutch oven; add sugar. Bring to full rolling boil; boil hard for 4 min-utes, stirring occasionally. Remove from heat; add pectin. Skim; stir 5 minutes. Pour in hot, scalded jars; seal. Makes six ½-pints.

KUMQUAT MARMALADE

4 cups water
1 pint fresh kumquats
2 medium oranges
3 cups sugar
1 tablespoon lemon juice

Put *half* of the water and *half* the fresh kumquats in blender container; blend till coarsely chopped. Pour into 6-quart kettle. Repeat.

Remove peel from oranges; scrape off excess white membrane. Quarter oranges, removing seeds. Add orange peel and orange to blender container; blend till peel is finely chopped. Add to kumquat mixture. Boil, uncovered, for 30 minutes.

Measure mixture (should be about 3 cups) into 3-quart saucepan. Stir in sugar. Return to heat. Bring to full rolling boil; boil hard till mixture sheets off spoon, about 4 to 5 minutes, stirring constantly. Stir in lemon juice. Seal in hot, scalded jars. Makes four ½-pints.

WINTER PRESERVES

1½ cups dried apricots
1 cup uncooked pitted prunes
5 cups water
1 large orange
1 8¾-ounce can crushed pineapple
5 cups sugar

Rinse apricots and prunes. Cover with 5 cups water in large saucepan. Simmer, covered, for 15 minutes; do not drain. Put *half* of the cooked fruit mixture in blender container; blend till coarsely chopped. Put mixture in large kettle. Repeat process.

Peel orange, reserving peel. Scrape off excess white membrane. Section orange over bowl to catch juice. Add orange sections with juice and orange peel to blender container; blend till orange peel is finely chopped.

Add chopped orange and peel, undrained pineapple, and sugar to mixture in kettle. Bring to boiling; reduce heat and boil till mixture is of desired consistency, stirring occasionally, about 25 minutes. Seal immediately in hot, scalded jars. Makes five ½-pint jars.

CRANBERRY PRESERVES

2 medium oranges
2 cups water
4 cups fresh cranberries
3¾ cups sugar

Peel oranges, reserving the peel of 1 orange. Cut orange into quarters; remove seeds. Place orange quarters and orange peel in blender container; blend till orange peel is finely chopped. Combine orange mixture and water in large kettle. Bring orange mixture to boiling; cover and cook slowly for 10 minutes.

Put *1 cup* of the cranberries in blender container; blend till coarsely chopped. Add to mixture in kettle. Repeat for remaining cranberries. Add sugar. Bring mixture to boiling, stirring till sugar dissolves. Boil hard, stirring constantly, till mixture sheets off metal spoon, about 6 to 7 minutes. Ladle into hot, scalded jars; seal. Makes five ½-pint jars.

Make and decorate a jar of Cranberry Preserves, Winter Preserves, Kumquat Marmalade, or Orange Marmalade for gifts.

CARE AND CLEANING

Keep your blender operating at peak efficiency by following a few basic procedures for its use and maintenance. Although each model will have some specific do's and don'ts listed in the manufacturer's instruction booklet accompanying it, many rules apply to all brands, old and new.

Use and Care

• Operate blender on a dry, clean surface. The dry surface is recommended for all electrical appliances, and the absence of crumbs keeps foreign material from getting into the blender mechanism.

• Be sure that blender container and cutting assembly rest firmly in base before turning on motor. If cutting assembly screws onto bottom of container, make sure the rubber sealing ring is in place and threaded base is screwed on correctly and tightly. If container should turn during processing, switch blender off and tighten screw band.

• Always cover blender before turning on motor. Place cover firmly on container and rest your hand lightly on the lid when starting the motor. If for some reason the lid is not on securely, your hand will prevent the lid from coming off the container.

• Do not remove container from base until the motor stops. Likewise, do not replace the container while the motor is running.

• When blending is completed, lift container straight up. If it does not lift easily, rock gently and lift up—do not twist.

• Transfer blended foods to another container for storage. This will keep your blender container free and ready to use.

• Avoid overtaxing the motor with heavy mixtures. When motor labors, try a higher speed or remove part of the contents and blend in smaller batches.

• If food becomes packed around blades, switch blender off and use a rubber spatula to dislodge food, or add several drops of liquid and complete blending.

• Use caution when adding ingredients while the motor is running. This will prevent undue spattering. If blender lid has a removable insert, ingredients can be added through this smaller opening. If the lid is a single unit, fit a piece of foil over top of blender container and cut an opening in the foil large enough to accommodate the food which is being added to the container.

• Switch blender off and wait for blades to stop turning before putting a spatula or other utensil in blender container. This not only prevents splashing of contents, but also prevents the possibility of catching the spatula in the blender. The exception to this rule is when blending a thick mixture and the vortex or whirlpool does not form. Then, use a narrow rubber spatula to push down the food from the sides of the container while the motor is running. Keep spatula close to sides of container to avoid blades.

• Check the manufacturer's instructions regarding how to add hot liquids. Some recommend allowing liquids to cool slightly before pouring into the container.

Cleaning Guide

• Wash blender container after each use. Fill 1/3 full with lukewarm water and add a small amount of detergent. Adjust lid on blender and run motor for a few seconds till blender is sparkling clean. Rinse, dry, and return the blender container to the motor base.

• If blender container has a removable cutting assembly, take it apart and wash it separately in the dishpan. Dry each part, reassemble, and return to motor base.

• Check blender manufacturer's instruction booklet before putting blender container in an automatic dishwasher.

• Never immerse motor base in water. Merely wipe chrome and outside of motor base with a clean, damp cloth; dry well. Also, since the motor is sealed it does not need to be lubricated unless so specified.

INDEX

94